Voices From Behind the Scenes

Teachers' Experiences in the Classroom Expressed through Poetry and Prose

Edited by
Valerie Knowles Combie

ASPECT Books
www.ASPECTBooks.com

World rights reserved. This book or any portion thereof may not be copied or reproduced in any form or manner whatever, except as provided by law, without the written permission of the publisher, except by a reviewer who may quote brief passages in a review.

This book is sold with the understanding that the publisher is not engaged in giving spiritual, legal, medical, or other professional advice. If authoritative advice is needed, the reader should seek the counsel of a competent professional

Front Cover: ccaetano/BigStock.com
Back Cover: iofoto.com/BigStock.com

Copyright © 2013 ASPECT Books
ISBN-13: 978-1-4796-0242-1 (Paperback)
ISBN-13: 978-1-4796-0243-8 (ePub)
ISBN-13: 978-1-4796-0244-5 (Kindle / Mobi)
Library of Congress Control Number: 2013912444

Published by

Table of Contents

Foreword v

I Am a Teacher 7

Open 9

Student Mediocrity 10

How Can I Teach You? 11

Educate 12

You Have Made a Difference 13

Educating Whom? What's the Sense? 16

Teaching Children 17

I Am What I Learn 18

The Statistic 19

Do I Have What it Takes? 20

Today's Teachers 21

Adolescent Dropouts 22

Confessions of a High School Marketing Teacher: A Day in the Life 24

For the Love of Grammar 29

A Place of Learning Gone Haywire 31

Teacher Reflections 33

The Teacher's Cry 34

The Gift of Teaching 35

A Challenging Student 37

Memorable Teaching Experiences 40

Richard, Redux 44

A Typical Day at the Writing Project 46

A Second Look 49

The Fisted Pebble: Teaching with an Open Heart and Hand 50

Spirit Writing 55

A Coach's Dilemma 59

Supporting Students for Literacy Success 66

Dough Boy 67

Confessions of A High School Marketing Teacher … I'm An Artist 70

A Story to Tell 71

That Day at Gardenville 75

Getting Through 77

A Whole New World 78

My Compatriots 79

Confessions of A High School Marketing Teacher: Teaching Is… 81

My Wondering 82

I Coming Over… 83

Why Are You Still Teaching? 89

Why Teach? 90

English as a Second Language 91

Just Not Interested? 96

Student Mediocrity 97

Students Achieving Higher Academic Standards 99

Drastic Measures 102

Whipped 104

A Soccer Story 107

The ABCs of a Good Teacher 110

Dear Mr. and Mrs. Taylor 111

The Homework Dilemma: Writings from a Frustrated Teacher 112

Acknowledgments 114

About the Authors 116

Foreword

In 2012, the Virgin Islands Writing Project (VIWP), an affiliate of the National Writing Project (NWP), and a partner of the Virgin Islands Department of Education and the University of the Virgin Islands, celebrated its tenth anniversary. For ten years, the VIWP has been working with teachers in both the St. Thomas/St. John District, and the St. Croix District of the Virgin Islands Department of Education, teaching teachers to teach writing in their classes. In the Summer Institute held each year, teachers are exposed to many strategies to teach writing, which they have been encouraged to apply in their classes. Although we have no documented evidence of improved scores on standardized tests, we would like to believe that the teacher consultants (TCs) have been making a difference in students' writing.

The poetry and prose included in this book document some of the experiences of TCs and other teachers in the Territory. We hope that these will present an insight into the work that teachers engage in daily. We hope that many teachers, among others, will read the experiences and insights in this book and be inspired.

The arrangement of poetry, followed by short stories, and then letters is a deliberate attempt to show that we engage in different modes of writing because we want to appeal to a wide variety of readers.

The authors' brief biographies are listed at the back of the book.

Please read and be inspired.

Valerie Knowles Combie, Ph.D.
Director, VIWP

I Am a Teacher

By Valerie Combie

Builders erect structures
Of aesthetic beauty and form
Engineers construct bridges and dams
Exotic designs to withstand any storm.
But I shape character
I develop young inquiring minds
That will outlast the strongest tower
Reproducing species in kind.

People gaze in amazement and awe
At the results of man's ingenuity and skill
They praise the discoveries of scientists, hurrah!
Whose advancements in medicine with hope fill.
I stimulate a child's quest for life
That desire to conquer self and learn to prepare
For the future by contributing to those in the strife
Of the battle that generates anger and fear.

The athletes command respect and fame
Flaunting their brawn, not necessarily brain
As they manipulate the rules of the game
Blanketed by wealth but not immune from pain.
But I instill moral values and love
Hearts filled with general care and empathy
Children as wise as serpents and harmless as doves
Who understand the golden rule's unlimited boundary.

The artist confounds the perception
With nameless flights of vision
Exemplified by bankers and financiers' imagination
As they manipulate data satisfying their passion.
I engage and encourage the masses of our youth
In meeting their objectives in their pursuit of truth

To maintain pride and dignity without losing the common touch
By helping others in need of so much.

Towering structures and exquisite monuments
Enhance our physical landscape
But they are temporary structures, food for social comment
Edifices of wood and stone, victims of the elements' rage.
But character is forever, extending beyond the grave
Influencing, motivating, touching lives
Creating a gargantuan ripple effect with the power to save
Those who have been battered in the strife.

So when people ask, "What do you do?"
Very proudly, I state, "I'm a teacher
An architect, a doctor, an engineer, a scientist, a counselor."
All combined in one creating structures, healing emotions
But most importantly, crafting characters
Imprints that will survive
Long after this physical life
That's why I am a teacher.

Open

By Elizabeth "Lisa" Beck

Open your eyes, teachers,
See what they need,
Explore the vast universe
And plant a seed.
Open your ears, teachers,
Hear what they yearn,
Search for opportunities
So they can learn.
Open your mouths, teachers,
Speak of the goal,
Tell the stories
Of successes untold.
Open your minds, teachers,
Help them to think,
Create a plan
To show them the link.
Open your hearts, teachers,
Show them you care,
Receive rewards,
Too many to compare.

Student Mediocrity

By Joan Paulus

An outgoing student advises an incoming student about what to expect in my reading class.
That little old lady in room 911
I really believe she thinks she is young
Her steps are brisk, her face is glad
I've often asked her if she ever gets mad.
Sometimes we'd wish that she would get sick
So we could all enjoy a good break.
Thank God I am now out of her class
So much stress wondering if I would pass.
I started the class well, you see,
Daily journal and sharing, you could depend on me.
In reading, I went from level one to three,
Then procrastinated, skipped classes, "limed" with my buddies.
As I look back now, I have a few regrets
But I cannot greet her with less than respect
For she continuously informed me of how I was losing
And my B dropped to C- of my own choosing.
In spite of all this I'll share with you some views
When you confront this little woman, better be on your cues
If you think a character trait is equal to one sentence
You will quickly learn you are lacking proper evidence.
You must include examples from the pages you have read
And before you know it, one sentence is four instead.
You will often hear the phrase, "Age appropriate language, please."
So "nice," "small," "big," "good," or "bad" consider them deceased.
If you mistakenly ask her the meaning of a word
She'll point to the dictionary, that special book for nerds,
"Take it up and show me your initiative for learning."
You'll find yourself embracing behaviors you've been shirking.
For the pieces of the portfolio you'll be guided along the way
Seeing that it is a project grade, stay focused! Do not stray!
Crucian proverbs, interaction, I enjoyed her class on the whole
That "A brain" she always said I had, was just on cruise control.

How Can I Teach You?

By Jesus Espinosa

When the odds are stocked up high against you,
How can I teach you?
When from the moment you try uttering your first words,
You were not taught or given the opportunity to properly formulate them.
How can I teach you?
With all the changes and legislation that keep teachers
Scrambling to find out to what degree you benefit, or are limited by what rules that are
    in effect,
How can l teach you?
When you started your journey in learning so long ago, that today everything seems to be
    now a given,
How can l teach you?
When you refuse to write or even read materials, because it's simpler to give everything in
    a handout,
And you need not bother to write from the blackboard,
How can l teach you
Basic concepts and fundamentals,
When iPhones, MP3s, and cell phones can translate for you all you want to learn and know?
How can l teach you?
The reality of life is that your interest is only in making fast money
And forgetting about your responsibilities to society.
How can l teach you
To realize that if you can't read and write
You won't learn how to be a leader, but a follower
And will fall for anything you hear, and do as you are told by someone else.
How can I teach you?

Educate

By Lorraine Cadet

(Sung to the tune of "Mary Had a Little Lamb.")

Reading is fun to do, fun to do, fun to do
Reading is fun to do the better reader you'll become
Writing is exploration, exploration, exploration
Writing is exploration; it is your thoughts on paper.
Listening is a critical skill, critical skill, critical skill
Listening is a critical skill, it helps you process information
They help you to succeed in school, succeed in school, succeed in school
They help you to succeed in school, so put them to good use
School is very good for you, good for you, good for you
School is very good for you, that's why you should stay in school.

You Have Made a Difference

By Valerie Combie

Invitational Summer Institute 2009
Has brought new meaning to my mind.
A special group of eleven
Invited, selected, chosen
You have given new meaning to diversity
Combining your talents, your gifts, and your creativity
You have made this year's institute great
Consistently on time, no one was significantly late
No interruptions by cell phone
Ringing
Demanding
Embarrassing
Defying the rules of courtesy.
You are teachers with a difference
Committed
Dedicated
Involved
Interested
In love
In love with the Master Teacher
In love with your work
In love with your students
In love with your support network
In rich combination
For your students' success, perfect fruition
You have made Summer Institute 2009
The best I've experienced at this time
And I want to thank you.
Victor, you are the VIWP's philosopher
Spewing gems of wisdom, provoking thoughts in others.
Glenda, always the wife of a preacher
So authentic, always a lover.
Patricia, your dramatical performances

Created images in our minds.
Susan, when given the choice,
You chose the Summer Institute
Which has made all the difference.
Carol, you've always been with us
Matching attractively, undisturbed
Sharing your academic pearls.
Catherine, so devoted to your task
So committed
But Sit Licie will always beckon with its charms.
Nancy, it's sad you had to go
That wasn't the plan.

John, we thought we'd have your wife and you
But you have proved that one is enough.
Yania, your calm composure exudes grace
We hope the Summer Institute has equipped you as you find your place.
Melonie, we'll hold you to your promise
To be our witness
Bringing friends and colleagues to the VIWP.
Nilaja, "Good day to you,"
You are well crafted
For the course you have charted.
Sharon, Fenella, Mary, Martha, Joan, and Veronica,
The VIWP's Summer Institute is richer
For the roles you've assumed
Facilitating
Coaching
Leading Writing Groups, Reading Groups
Assisting with technology
Entertaining.
Thanks to you all,
But this is not the end.
Let's meet in September
For Continuity on St. Thomas/St. John, St. Croix
In this new marriage
We're like a horse and carriage
So let's stay together TCs, Teacher Consultants, indeed

Be prepared for Inservice
Professional Development in schools
You've been trained
Now you'll train others
Teachers training teachers
That's our motto, our pledge, our rule.
And now, as we say farewell,
The future, only time will tell.
But you have surely made a difference!
God bless you all!

Educating Whom? What's the Sense?

By Jesus Espinosa

When I gave you knowledge, you refused to take it.
When I showed you how, you would turn your head from looking.
How is it then that I am educating you?
What's the sense in trying to teach you about your tomorrow?
Educating whom?
You!
What's the sense?
You would not take learning seriously.
You would not take directives about your task correctly,
So what's the sense?
You don't appreciate the time it takes for me to prepare for you.
When will you learn that life is more than what you see?
Educating whom?
People whose minds are closed to growth and development will never succeed.
What's the sense if you believe that only internet, ipad, and iphone can be your teachers?
You may have no future once you choose this road of digital speed with no promises.
Reading and writing are two fundamentals of learning, so why not try?
The choices you make will always determine how far you develop in life.
Educating whom?
What's the sense if you don't want to learn?

Teaching Children

By Anny Prescott

T – Thoughtful
E – Energetic
A – Attentive
C – Comforting
H – Helpful
I – Impartial
N – Noble
G – Giving

C – Creative
H – Hyperactive
I – Inquisitive
L – Lovable
D – Dependable
R – Reliable
E – Ever present
N – Noisy

I Am What I Learn

By Valerie Combie

I learned, very early, that love is a stabilizing force that keeps us grounded.
I learned to share.
I learned responsibility.
I learned to be sensitive.
I learned loyalty.
I learned patience.
I learned to be seen and not heard.
I learned if I make my bed, I must lie in it.
I learned "birds of a feather flock together,"
And if I "lie with dogs I'll rise with fleas."
I learned that "manners maketh man."
I learned that "a rolling stone gathers no moss,"
And "still waters run deep."
I learned to appreciate beauty.
I learned that people all over the world are the same,
And if one person hurts, we all hurt.
I learned to laugh heartily, lose graciously, and love sincerely,
Because those are the elements of a life well lived.

The Statistic

By Abigail Martyr

I hugged my textbook closer to my body,
As I walked down the hall in my oversized sweater;
The carefree laughter of classmates and friends
Drifted around me as if in a dream,
Reminiscent of a time, not too long ago,
When the world was mine for the taking.
Who would have thought that all innocence would be lost?
Or that a walk down the hall would feel like walking the plank,
When my heart threatened to stop at the sound of a whisper,
Afraid that my secret has already been discovered?
How will I face the days to come?
How long can I go without telling my mom?
'Cause like her—and my grandma before—
I am now a statistic…
ANOTHER TEENAGE MOTHER

Do I Have What it Takes?

By Avril Hart

I want to be a teacher; what will it take?
I want to be a teacher; do I have what it takes?
I want to be a teacher; tell me what it takes!
They tell me to expect days of laughter and of tears;
Days to stand my ground and days to surrender my fears;
Days to be creative and days to inspire creativity.
Do I have what it takes?

I need four years of college to acquire that knowledge.
It will cost a lot of money and mom said "I don't have it, honey."
I want to be a teacher, what am I going to do?
The government provides for people like you.
I will need to keep my grades up just to qualify;
So I'd better study harder or my dreams will die.

Now that I am a teacher, do I have what it takes,
To believe in the possibilities each child embraces?
Do I REALLY have what it takes?

Today's Teachers

By Joan Paulus

Vibrant seekers, facing the challenges
Of those entrusted in their care
At times they traverse from distant shores to partake of the brief respite
The invitational summer institute offers.
And so they arrive, sharing honestly of themselves
Reflecting, perhaps, on their original call
To a vocation whose rewards are not so readily visible.
Techno masters, comfortably forging innovative means of communicating
Lessons of life and living borne of disciplined forerunners,
Living symbols of hope and possibilities
To an otherwise oblivious lot whose dreams may have been tarnished
By imposed economic, social, and psychological barriers
Which have rendered them antagonists in the game of life
May this summer be like a banquet
As we partake of the foods of collegiality
Sharing the sweet wines of our dedication and commitment
To nurture, strengthen, and guide our brothers and sisters
Of our solitary human family.

Adolescent Dropouts

By Camille Santiago

I've made a decision
What a decision I've made!
At school my teachers are screaming
My time is mine not yours
My homework is never finished
My test scores keep growing low
I've made a decision
What decision have I made?
Am I a boy? Am I a girl?
Who cares about my gender?
I had a friend
Got very close
And when I least expected
Had a family on my own
I've made a decision
What decision have I made?
Nobody cares
Nobody is trying
To hear my cry
I feel like dying
I'm in a box
With my deceptions
I tried to grow
And I got your rejection
I've made a decision

What decision have I made?
I can't go to school tomorrow
I'm leaving my books behind
My father drinks
My mom is out
Who's going to feed me?
Who will help out?
I've made a decision
What decision have I made?
I QUIT!

Confessions of a High School Marketing Teacher: A Day in the Life

By Stefanie Samuel

I barely hear my cell alarm sing
Stretching, rolling, trying to find my zing.

What day is it? Thoughts drown my head
Why couldn't it have been a holiday?
I could stay in bed instead.

Blast on the radio to get in the mood
I'm sure my neighbors say I'm rude.

I drag myself from under the sheets
Into the shower and brush my teeth.

Iron my clothes and pack my lunch
Slip on my heels and hurry to beat the crunch.

Jump in my car and reverse out the gate
See the time 7:20 a.m.; hope I'm not late.

Driving in traffic, I think to myself
What am I teaching today? I'll pull an activity off the shelf.

Into the lot at my-self-designated space,
I walk up the sidewalk into the office looking for the case.

The case is gone; I guess I'm late
I look for the sign-in sheet that I hate.

I check my box to see if the copies were made
No copies there! Why don't they do the jobs for which they're paid?

I guess no copies means a change in plan
Out of the office through the door into teenage land.

"Mawning! Mawning!" The monitors say
"Buenos morning," I respond (how I greet the day)

Up the stairs, and it begins "Morning, Ms. Samuel"
"Morning," I reply out of wind. "How are you?" "I am well."

I make my rounds down the hall
Beck, Petersen, and Lockhart saying hi to all

Searching for my keys, I dig into my bag
Why do they fall to the bottom? "Open the door," my students nag!

J210 is where my world comes alive
Into lessons and engagement we will dive.

I sit at my desk to begin the day
"The principal wants you outside," the students say.

Barely at the desk, I go outside to see
My principal smiling at me.

"Ms. Samuel, the board is visiting today
We would like some students to show them the way."

"How long has he known this?" came to my head
I shook it off and said "No problem," instead.

Back into the classroom I search for a student
One who will be polite, courteous, and prudent

"Jessica, see me; I have a task for you
And you, Michael, you may join her too."

I give the students instructions at hand
Then back to my desk for the lesson planned.

OK, let's begin with our class activity
"Ms. Samuel, not today, we have no A/C."

I look at the ceiling. It is kind of hot
I can feel this day will be shot.

Look who rolls in twenty minutes late
Another student with no I. D. at the gate.

Here comes another: "To Whom It May Concern:" said the note
"My son woke up late," the parent wrote.

I'm sick of late notes, I want to scream
But put the note down and a smile I beam.

Back to the activity on this day
Break up in groups for a game to play.

I read the instructions loud and clear
Repeat and retell for those who didn't hear.

We play the game and all love it.
"Today is fun. The game is a hit."

Class is over rings the bell
"Monday is a test! Study well!"

I say my daily quote: "Do choose the positive…"
And give them pointers on how to live

The next class rushes in with morning greetings
Some complain about chairs and seating.

Who took my chair was the "cry"
"Your parents pay for a seat, not a chair," I reply.

Seventeen more students coming down the hall
Screaming, playing, as if this is a mall.

Into class I greet them as they enter
I clear my mind and find my center.

"A parent outside the room to see you, Ms. S"
Another interruption, what a mess!

I grab my grade book to go outside
Whose mom is this? Looking for the student trying to hide.

"My name is Michelle; I came to see how Jimmy is in school
Because at home he performs the fool."

Jimmy has been great in class
But only does enough to pass.

I think if he applies himself more
He'll be more excited when he comes through the door.

I think as a parent you must be involved
And the problems at home will be resolved.

Jimmy is a good student really above
All he needs is tender care and love.

I bid the parent good day and escorted Jimmy in
The students are still in their seats working instead of playing.

I smile at myself to see them engaged
Instead of stifled like animals in a cage.

Five more minutes and then its lunchtime
I brought my lunch because I don't have a dime.

I say my I love yous as the students leave
Check my email, my eyes couldn't believe.

I had a department meeting; I totally forgot
I pack my lunch and walk to another classroom that was hot.

Agenda for the day; Ms. Beck hands us a list
I need to use the restroom right after this.

We exchange, discuss, and ideas we share
Speak about things to do for next school year.

It's 3rd period already and students file in
I hunt for my keys that I'm always losing.

Back in class the students settle in
"Pardon the interruption," the voice begins.

"Teachers please excuse 11th graders for a meeting."
Some of these counselors really need a beating.

"Eleventh graders, you heard the announcement
Check you emails; I'll send the homework by attachment."

I keep forgetting the need to go to the restroom
And tell the custodian to come to my class to "pass the broom."

I'll go to the rest room during my prep
Then come back and prepare my lesson plans in depth.

School is over and it was a long day
Another day where I earned my pay.

I Lock the door and turn off the lights
Down the hall and say my good nights.

Down the stairs and through the gate
I reflect on the day and for tomorrow I can't wait.

For the Love of Grammar

By Valerie Combie

"Amo, amas, amat
Amamus, amatis, amant."
"I love, you love, he/she/it loves
We love, you love, they love."
Thus goes the Latin version
Of grammatical conjugation
The rule requires diligence
If one's speech must reflect intelligence.
Verb conjugation
Eliminates subjugation
While it manifests transformation
In one's disposition.
What is grammar?
What are the rules we follow?
Why can I not be creative
And exercise my prerogative to be inventive?
There's inventive spelling,
Inventive reading
Why can I not introduce
An inventive grammar without any excuse?
I may be cute and stun my audience
With conjugations of such brilliance
Such as: I goes, you goes, he/she/it go
You was, they was, I were.
You acknowledge my non compos mentis.
The object of the preposition
Is not the subject; there's no opposition
Therefore, it is selectively known
That after the preposition comes the object pronoun.
Relative pronouns are singular
The replacing pronoun must agree in number, case, and gender
With its antecedent
When anyone, someone, or everyone is meant.

With a linking verb, think predicate nominative
And eliminate the idea of the objective
"It is I," "It is he," "It is she, "It is we"
May sound funny, but are correct, you'll agree.
When talking about agreement
There must be no sign of dissent
As subjects and verbs are the same
Whether in church, in court, or in a game.
The auxiliary is simply the helping verb
That connects with other words
To create fluency
That's the work of the auxiliary.
"She has seen" introduces the past participle.
No need to mention a definite or indefinite article
Just follow the rule
And give great credit to your school.
When the grammatistes of Greco –Rome
Instructed students in grammata at home
They became grammatikos, literate
Which may not make them more considerate.
But the term "grammar" is not abused
"Grammar School" is being used
To reflect the Greco-Roman intent
To teach grammar to young twigs before they're bent.
Teach subject verb agreement
Teach proper verb conjugation
Enforce appropriate diction
So that students can be enlightened
As they wander through the academic maze
Applying grammatical principles all their days
Long live our grammatikos!
Their knowledge they'll expose
And put to an end
The wave of crime and killing men
An existential leap, you may say
But there's a great relationship this way
Between our grammar
And our behavior!

A Place of Learning Gone Haywire

By Esther Burroughs

Feeling so drained at the end of a school day
For most of the time spent telling students to obey
The lessons and skills seem to be going no where
The students appear to be giving a deaf ear.

No interest or concern for the lessons presented
So they focus on their own agenda instead
Cursing each other and sometimes the teacher, too
To get them to listen seems so difficult to get through.

Never thought it would come to this
A place for learning with such violently shift
The inappropriate behavior so hard to tame
Others on the outside think teachers are to be blamed.

It's so hard to get them where they ought to be
Imagine the offensive words they say to others and me
No respect or regard for their Creator or man
And when it's time to work, they never understand.

Their voices are loud, vicious, and aggressively crude
Some are disruptive and plain out rude
Respect for faculty and staff is out of control
They seem to have no specific desire or goal.

This behavior has truly taken a toll on teachers
For sometimes the day seems nothing but a failure
The attitude has gone bizarre and rocks the soul
Hope they will someday be a good role-model of this world.

It hurts to see them go the wrong way,
Sometimes all we can do is to pray.
They may change for the better someday,
And the place of learning once again will be okay.

Although some students can be a challenge and certainly not fun
Don't give up until the job of reaching at least one is done
Never mind if the days may seem haywire or wild
Remember, there is a sea of greatness in every child.

Teacher Reflections

By Mary Edwards

I am a
Bumbling Idiot,
Tongue Tied Teacher,
Stupid Student.
Imagine how a child reader sometimes feels.
I am
Behind,
Unfinished,
All mixed up.
Imagine how a child writer feels sometimes.
I cannot
Think of a word to write,
Create a poetic piece,
Come up with a catchy title.
Imagine how a student sometimes feels.
A student needs Teaching.
A student needs Time.
A student needs Encouragement.
The teacher reader-writer,
The student reader-writer,
Both need nurturing!

The Teacher's Cry

By Veronica Prescott

Getting ready for school
With my grit and usual tools
I come with much anticipation,
Expecting to grab my students' attention.

With new strategies and skills in hand
I'm ready to amend the usual plan
Confident with research, the lesson will bloom
I'm certain the materials will be consumed

But the classroom is a nightmare
Teachers working in despair
Disrespect and uncertainties
Are the norm of new policies.

Profanity parades the schools
A total disregard of campus rules.
Whether in classroom or on campus ground
They are oblivious to who is around!

Defeated and deactivated
When efforts are so depreciated
The crude challenges of each day
Do drive educators away.

The Gift of Teaching

By Kimarie Engerman

When my 11th grade Honors English teacher introduced herself on the first day of classes, she said in addition to teaching at my high school, she taught English part-time at the University of the Virgin Islands (UVI). The minute she said that, something in my heart leaped. I immediately knew what my career aspiration was, to become a college professor at UVI. The funny thing is that I passed UVI every day, but never stepped foot on the campus. Nevertheless, she made me realize that my calling in life was to teach and inspire college students.

After completing my first semester in the classroom as a Preparing Future Faculty Fellow, a non-traditional student gave me a memento that stated, "To teach is to change a life." The accompanying card went on to state how thankful the student was for having me as her instructor. She acknowledged her many weaknesses and addressed how I helped her overcome those weaknesses. The student concluded by stating that I changed her life. For this reason, teaching to me is a gift. It is not limited to providing students with knowledge. An effective teacher helps students recognize their abilities to overcome challenges needed to be successful.

Furthermore, teaching involves communicating the information in such a way that students develop a deep understanding of the concepts. The fruit of your labor is exhibited when students can recognize the concepts you taught them and apply those concepts to their everyday living. More importantly, teaching involves creating an excitement for the subject matter even when you are not excited about the subject. An example of this is when I teach *History and Systems of Psychology*. I am not a historian, nor am I overly excited about the history of psychology. However, when I enter the classroom, it is not about me. It is all about the students learning the information. Most of the students enter *History and Systems of Psychology* knowing it will be boring and are just there to either fulfill their psychology requirement or get somewhat prepared for the Psychology Graduate Record Exam.

I remember one spring semester when I taught *History and Systems of Psychology*, I had a student, DKA, who sat in on the first day of classes, without registering for the class. DKA had taken a few classes with me before, so he was already familiar with my teaching style. However, DKA knew the subject matter for this particular class was going to be boring, so he wanted to see what I was offering before he wasted his time taking a class he would drop at the end of the week. Needless to say, I somehow managed to capture DKA's interest and he decided to register for the course. At the end of the semester, DKA felt this was the best course he had taken at the university. Furthermore, the following semester while attending graduate school, I got an email correspondence from DKA that stated, "One of my professors sometimes refers to me as "my little psychology historian." Another often says, "Mr. DKA, tell us something interesting about..... I still believe that this is the best course in Psychology. Thank you again for making the past events and characters jump to life."

As you can see, teaching requires creativity. You must think outside of the box and develop activities that are meaningful to students. Learning is valuable when students can relate to the information that is being learned. While teaching the class, I didn't realized it was having such a strong impact on DKA. All I knew is that it is boring to me and I needed to make it fun.

Unfortunately, DKA is not the typical student I encounter. He was a serious student who took meticulous notes. His notes were not limited to lecture materials, but also included general classroom announcements or discussions. A student like DKA could possibly intimidate any professor who is not confident or competent. Yet on the other hand, a student like DKA is a breath of fresh air in a class where it is obvious that the students are not motivated to succeed.

Speaking about the lack of motivation in students, my greatest challenge so far in my teaching career was when I taught Freshman Development Seminar (FDS) for the first time. Teaching those freshmen exposed me to a world I never knew existed. In the "world" I existed in prior to teaching FDS, students knew the script that was required when taking a course in college. The script entailed the student being punctual for class, completing and submitting homework assignments in the appropriate format, participating in class discussions, and just generally contributing to the learning experiences of everyone present in the classroom. Well, I was in for a rude awakening. Who did I think I was bringing such high standards to FDS? The students were upset with me for starting the class on time. (There was even this one student whose off-campus job ended the same time my class started.) The students felt I should have given them a 5-to-10 minutes grace period before starting class. Also, the students could not understand why my section had assignments, but some of the other sections did not. Needless to say, teaching FDS that semester made me question whether or not teaching was really for me. Despite the fact that I wondered if I was the problem with my high expectations, I did not lower my standards. Towards the end of the semester, I noticed that some students finally got the message and made improvements.

When that semester ended, I vowed never to teach FDS again. I guess it is true that one should not say never because I got roped into teaching it the following year. All I can honestly say is that experience is indeed our best teacher. The second time around was not as stressful as the first time. I maintained my standards. However, I accepted the fact that freshmen are "special" and require more nurturing than my upperclassmen.

In retrospect, I am glad I had that challenging experience with FDS. It made me realize that in order to be an effective teacher, I have to be flexible. My classes will always start on time; however, I need to remain mindful of my approach because students bring different needs and expectations into the classroom. Some students are well prepared and others need to be immediately referred to the appropriate resource office on campus. More importantly, it is my responsibility as a teacher to capture my students' attention and motivate them to learn. Again, teaching is a gift.

A Challenging Student

By Joan Paulus

The student who remains the freshest in my memory is the one I will refer to as Joel, probably because of his outward boldness and uncanny knack for devising pranks and schemes to avoid class work and to seek attention. He was a handsome mixture of black and Hispanic, and a seventeen-year-old high school freshman among a group of mostly fourteen- and fifteen-year-olds. It was my final semester before retiring as a reading teacher from the Virgin Islands Department of Education, February to June of 2011.

From the second day of class, Joel's actions indicated that I was in for some challenges. While I was speaking he would start singing, or jump out of his seat and perform some dance movements much to the entertainment of his classmates, totally ignoring classroom rules. My first shock came on the first week when he danced in the class and created an impromptu song expressing his desire to have sex with me, deliberately ignoring the fact that a student was sharing his journal entry for the day. So he would not think that this behavior would be tolerated, I took the matter to the assistant principal who scheduled a meeting with his father the following morning. Joel came to my class later that day to apologize and inform me, quite happily, that he would be suspended for two days. What this incident signaled to me was perhaps the student did not want to be in school.

When confronted with a challenger like Joel, to determine if I am sane or not, I usually obtain a copy of his schedule and consult with all his teachers to get a feel of his comportment in their classes. The reports were all the same of not trying, not completing nor turning in assignments, but the outrageous behaviors I experienced with him were not evident. In their classes he was equivalent to a silent non- worker who was not even trying to get ahead.

When he returned to class, I noticed that the dancing and singing were less frequent and whenever Joel sat with Jasmine, a junior, he made some efforts to complete some assignments. A few times he sat at a desk in front of me and informed me not to worry about him because he "got things under his wings." When asked to educate me as to the meaning of the phrase he explained, "I have skills." He became the subject of a poem on which I elaborated that summer at the Virgin Islands Writing Project's Invitational Summer Institute.

Signs of Hope

He is always the last to enter the door, in the midst of journal writing he'll arrive for sure

IPod blasting calypso or reggae, singing to high heaven while dancing in his way.

Conferencing, counselor intervention I've tried to no avail

Behavioral letters written to me, I've decided to curtail

After his second suggestion should this happen another time

Fifty pushups in front of the class, to him I must assign.

No more attention will I pay to his lofty grand entrance

For when there is no audience, there'll be no performance.

Realizing he was no more the centerpiece of attention

He decided to put more focus on some of his lessons

A few assignments and some homework he managed to submit

This lad had much potential if he'd only stick to it.

"I can do the work, but I just don't want to," he'd sing.

"I'm a survivor! I've got things under my wings.

I can drive heavy equipment, do auto body, and landscaping, too.

And a few other skills I'm not yet ready to share with you.

I do not complete assignments in my other classes either

So I do not expect passes at the end of the semester.

But don't worry, Ms. Paulus, I'm a survivor you will see."

It was a pleasant summer surprise when I met him by the tree

Dressed in uniform that Wednesday, waiting for a taxi.

"Is that you, Ms. Paulus?" We exchanged pleasantries.

He was enrolled in two classes for credit recovery.

Joel did not obtain a passing grade for my class because he did not fulfill the requirements. I saw him several mornings waiting for a taxi during the summer, and during the first and second semesters of the following school year, at least until March of 2012. I never saw him after that. I wonder about him every once in a while – if he is still on St. Croix or if he relocated to St. Thomas where his mother lives; if he attends night school; if he is employed or not? My interface with him did leave me questioning how many of our male students are in a similar predicament and what intervention strategies are being employed to lessen the increasing numbers.

Memorable Teaching Experiences

By Denis Griffith

Two of my most interesting and memorable experiences have been with two of my university students who are blind. One walks with a cane, and the other has learned to move around without a cane. When they entered my first class, the other students who did not know them before wondered how they would be able to complete the program. The challenge was how they would write; how they would do research papers; how they would take final examinations; how they would make presentations, and defend their theses.

The first lesson that I learned from these students was that they were determined to earn their degrees. We began an adventure in learning. The first student, Carmen, was not born blind. She had obtained a bachelor's degree; she was a teacher in Texas, and she is a confident young woman.

When we were introducing ourselves in class, Carmen related how she got up one morning, opened her eyes and could not see anything. She was in total darkness. After several visits to different doctors, they confirmed that she had gone blind. She had inherited diabetes, which caused her blindness. Carmen had to learn to live with her blindness.

During class I allowed her to tape record all our lessons so that she could replay them at home. For her writing, she used a ruler to keep her lines straight, but her writing was a bit stringy at first, but she gradually improved on her penmanship. To overcome the illegibility of her writing, I would ask her to verbalize what she was trying to convey in her writing. She was articulate. She could answer the questions adequately. The other students in class encouraged her. Gradually her handwriting became more legible.

The most challenging part of her studies was writing her thesis. After our preliminary discussion about her proposal, Carmen hired an undergraduate student to be her reader and her typist. The student would search for topics and read articles that Carmen recommended. After the first draft of her proposal was written, the undergraduate student could not continue to read and type for Carmen due to her own course load.

In order for Carmen to stay on track we sought help from the Virgin Islands University Center for Excellence in Developmental Disabilities (VIUCEDD). The VIUCEDD office has technology to assist students with disabilities. There she got the technological assistance that she needed. As her advisor, I also became her mentor. I had to spend time typing parts of her study. We were also able to tap into "related services" that were available at the Government Office for the Disabled. (Related Services are services beyond special education that advance individualized education program goals and improve access to interventions including therapy, classroom aides, transportation, and special equipment). In Carmen's case we got the special equipment. Her parents are very supportive and her father drives her everywhere.

In our administration classes we spent time discussing topics on special education. We studied the Individuals with Disabilities Act of 1990 (Public Law or PL, 101-476) and the updated Individuals with Disabilities Education Improvement Act of 2004 [PL 108-446]. As administrators and aspiring administrators, we discussed and learned the current jargon on special education. We learned about (1) Individualized Education Program (IEP); (2) Free appropriate public education (FAPE); (3) the Federal Family educational rights and privacy acts (FERPA); (4) Least restrictive environment. Those discussions helped the administrators to more clearly understand their roles as they tried to educate students in their respective schools.

Carmen had invaluable information on those topics and she would take the lead in those discussions. As the class researched topics on special education, everyone became knowledgeable about what it meant "to provide education in the least restrictive environment." I became more aware of what it meant to make "accommodations" or "modifications" for students with disabilities. I modeled to the other students how to be supportive and nonjudgmental of others.

As she continued to work on her thesis, I was able to make corrections and suggestions on her jump drive. I made a backup copy of everything that she wrote. With the assistance of Dr. Valerie Combie, an English professor and second reader, I was able to help Carmen submit her proposal to the Department of Education for approval to conduct her study on *Perceptions of the Academic Performance of LEP Students at the Arthur A. Richards Junior High School, St. Croix, USVI*. Carmen was able to successfully defend her thesis. The Counselor, who was the examiner, was fascinated that Carmen could answer all the questions that he asked. On Sunday, May 2007, Carmen graduated with her Master of Arts in Educational Leadership. When she received her diploma, I was able to escort her off the stage to her seat. At the end of the Commencement, Governor John deJongh told me: "That was a wonderful thing you did back there."

I am proud to say that Carmen was chair of the Best Beginnings Conference held in the Great Hall on the Albert A. Sheen Campus. Despite her blindness, Carmen continues to be an advocate for students. She is a resource teacher at the Arthur A. Richards Junior High School in Frederiksted, St. Croix. On Al Roker's radio show on St. Croix, Carmen was asked who was her favorite teacher I was honored to be chosen by her as one of the teachers of the year.

The other student is Willie. When Willie joined the Master of Educational Leadership program, he had already earned a bachelor's degree and a master's degree in Physical Education from Florida Agriculture and Machinery University (FAMU). Willie lost his sight when he was 19 years old. He suffers from optic atrophy, which he inherited from his mother. He has peripheral vision. He is legally blind. After he lost his sight, he had to go to the school for the blind where he learned Braille and mobility skills. He can walk without a cane. He explained that he had to memorize landmarks, people's voices, bodily shapes and how to walk on the grass and the sidewalk without a cane.

For the most part, Willie depends on his memory. Willie says that he found classes challenging because he has to memorize almost everything. He had to develop a new learning style. He changed from being a visual learner to an auditory learner and then to a kinesthetic learner.

During his course of study, Willie spent a considerable amount of time in the library. We had some thought-provoking discussions on many topics, and in particular, on his thesis topic. Because of his great desire to pursue the degree and his determination to succeed, many people volunteered to assist him. Willie read widely. As he told me, one of the librarians, Elroy, helped him to search for topics. Another IT professional, Marthious Clavier, helped him to set his data on Excel.

With the assistance of Dr. Combie, I was able to help him get his proposal, *Perceptions of Teachers and Administrators in the Two Public High Schools on St. Croix, USVI, toward Inclusion*, approved. Apart from the educational leadership courses, Willie also enrolled in business classes and business statistical courses to cement what he learned in our basic research classes. When I asked him what was the most challenging thing he faced during his studies, he responded that making a PowerPoint presentation was most challenging. To overcome this, he had someone prepare his slides, and then had someone in the class read the points and he elaborated on each point.

His next challenge was to demonstrate to those who doubted his ability that he had what it takes to succeed. He became a very forceful speaker. Willie earned his Master of Arts degree in Educational Leadership in 2009. From his thesis he has made presentations to the VIUCEDD Board. He is currently a board member of the VIUCEED and the Governor's Developmental Disability Council (DDC). He is now on his second of a six-year term.

Willie is a Physical Education teacher at the Eulalie Rivera Elementary School. His students have won 16 Most Valuable Player medals in track and field and his teams have won six national (territorial championships).

He is currently married to an attorney. He celebrated two years of marriage on June 18, 2013.

Lessons Learned

These two students were determined to succeed. They had challenging times, but persevered to the end. When a professor or teacher is willing to work with students and encourage them and give the support and make the necessary accommodations, the students will succeed. There were times when both of them were in my classes simultaneously.

On Wednesday, November 25, 2009, I was correcting students' assignments and had a hemorrhage in my right eye, which resulted in my loss of sight in that eye. I thought that I was working too hard and I was tired. I went to the restroom, washed my face and tried to continue correcting, but my right eye had no vision. Praise to God, I could still see in my left eye. I drove home, drank some Tylenol and went to bed. There was no pain in my eye. I just could not see with it. Since Thursday was Thanksgiving Day, no private doctors' offices were opened. When I went to the Vision Center the following Monday, the doctor who attended to me said that I had dry eyes and gave me some drops, but two days after, my eyes began to irritate. After my second visit, they discovered that I did have a hemorrhage.

I drew inspiration from both Carmen and Willie. I reasoned that these two students had shown me how to cope and I would manage. Thanks to my wife and Dr. Assefa who did laser surgery on my right eye, I was able to recover sight in that eye. Both Carmen and Willie were concerned when they heard about this dilemma. Carmen called to find out how I was doing. Willie comes to my office every other week to chat and engage me in discussion of his varies topics.

Richard, Redux

By Rosalyn Rossignol

When I met Richard Smith, he would have been sixteen or seventeen. I'm going to say sixteen because he seemed so young, like the youngest in my class of juniors at Antilles School, a private K-12 school located on St. Thomas in the US Virgin Islands. His hair was a cap of dark curls and he often came to class sporting his volleyball jersey, something that should have told me how much he cared about the sport, but I was, as a relatively inexperienced high school teacher, too focused on surviving things like lunch duty and parking lot duty and the expectation that I would give students demerits for things like wearing their skirts too short or chewing gum in class. My PhD in English and previous experience teaching college-level students had ill-prepared me for such activities. Richard, who was small for his age, sort of got lost in the general boisterousness of his classmates. His academic performance was middling; his attitude to his studies, lackadaisical. He sat in the back of the classroom and chatted endlessly with another student whose name escapes me now but who would, the following year, forever change Richard's life in ways that I could not have imagined.

Some students in that class, like the students a year ahead of them, would get into first-class universities with full scholarships. Many of them would graduate with multiple honors. Richard, I felt certain, would graduate. I had no idea if he had any ambition to attend university, or where he thought of applying. He seemed, of his classmates, the least academically serious. I am ashamed to say that instead of reaching out to him, even though this was a small school where I taught small classes, I concentrated my efforts and my attention on the students who, by virtue of their serious attitude and high marks, seemed to me to deserve it.

In the middle of that year, which was my second year teaching high school, I decided I just couldn't do it anymore and resigned, leaving behind Richard and the rest of the kids in my English literature class, as well as the other students I taught. After about a year recuperating from my high school experience, I began teaching at the University of the Virgin Islands. During that year, Richard Smith became a senior in high school. At the end of his senior year, he went out partying with some of his friends, and fell asleep in the back seat of one friend's car. That friend, who was driving while intoxicated, crashed into a tree. The accident broke Richard's neck.

Richard was life-flighted to a hospital in Miami where he spent a long time in a coma. When he woke up he was a quadriplegic, and had to start learning how to live his life without the use of his arms and legs. The next time I saw Richard he was rolling into my classroom at the University of the Virgin Islands in his motorized wheelchair. I had known he would be coming but nothing could have prepared me for the sight that now burned itself onto my corneas, the image of a severely disabled young man struggling to make his way in a culture that values physical beauty and physical prowess so highly. It made me want to cry. But that was before I came to know the new Richard. In the course of the semester, and to my great surprise, Richard consistently produced the best work in the class. He missed a few classes, sure, and I had to make special arrangements for him to take his final outside of class, but his enthusiasm and dedication to learning never failed to impress me. I understand, as someone who has come to know and care about Richard, that what happened to him was a terrible tragedy, as well as an injustice. (The young man who was driving the car escaped unscathed.) Richard could easily have become embittered and given up on life, shutting himself away from those who would stare at him in pity as he makes his way to his classes. Instead he has forged bravely ahead, excelling in his classes (his overall GPA is 3.59), and providing a shining example to others who face lesser obstacles in their daily lives. For these qualities, Richard is one student who will always inspire me, and whom I will never forget.

A Typical Day at the Writing Project

(Told from the Perspective of a Pencil)

By Sharon Charles

Wow! What a relief! Finally I can have some peace. It is summer time, and I am free. You will never imagine how thrilled I am. But wait! It's Wednesday, June 20, 2012, and it is relatively early. I can hear footsteps coming my way. I had better conceal myself. Maybe someone is coming to abuse me again.

I peep from the corner of my little bed, and I can hear the footsteps getting louder. They are closer now. I look up and see a beautiful black woman entering the room. She is looking around rather suspiciously. She has stacks of paper in her hand, and she places them on a desk near the back of the room. She steps quietly to the front of the room and places some other items on a table. I am not sure what these are, but I am curious. Before I could unravel this mystery, in walk a few others. They call this woman "Valerie." The women have a business-like expression on their faces. I wonder what they will be doing here.

Before long there is more talking and laughing in the room. This place is getting crowded! Maybe I should have tried to escape when the first woman walked in. I was so foolish to stay in my little corner and trying to play detective. Now it seems as if I am trapped. I cannot come out of hiding now. I am not even dressed well enough to be seen in public. I will just sit here quietly and listen.

Shh! Someone mentions something about writing. They are rearranging desks in the room. These people must be crazy. Why would they leave the comfort of their homes and come to a place like this so early in the morning just to talk about writing? They seem to have a problem. Why don't they just text each other, or better yet connect on facebook? Oh, I get it. They are teachers. They are here to write. As if interrupting my thoughts, the lady called Valerie walks to the front of the room.

"Good morning," she said. "It's 8:30. May we all stand and sing our VIWP theme song?"

"VIWP theme song?" I asked myself silently.

This is getting interesting. First, I thought they were going to write, but Valerie, who seems to be in charge, is asking them to sing. Nevertheless, they comply and sing rather lustily. It sure looks like some of them even sang from memory. I have never heard that song before. They say it was written by someone called Fenella Cooper.

Seconds later, Valerie mentions something about reading logs from last year. Someone named Joan is identified as the culprit. She meticulously takes out some papers and begins reading. She recounts the activities of the last day of the 2011 Summer Institute. Valerie also reads her logs. These people are really strange! Can you imagine waiting a whole year for information? After the reading, Valerie announces the loggers for today. Two women named Sharon and Charlene are named to keep a record of today's events.

"Events?" I questioned myself.

I wonder how long they plan to be here abusing my space and annoying my mind with this writing. Before I could complete my thought, to my surprise, Valerie tells everyone to introduce him/herself. I peep out of my corner to see their faces. Most of them are women. They say their names and mention where they work. Soon Valerie asks them to reflect on the question, "What have I gotten myself into by coming to the Virgin Islands Writing Project's Summer Institute (VIWP)?" She continues, "What are your plans for the next 15 days of the VIWP? How will this affect you for the rest of your life?" She gives the group 5 minutes to compose their thoughts on paper. When given an opportunity to share their responses many say they want to become better writers so that they could help their students. Others want to collaborate with peers, get an opportunity to soar, get an opportunity to write, get their work critiqued, and learn ideas and strategies that they can incorporate into their classrooms. Others want to become advocates for VIWP.

It seems like these folks have some great expectations! Valerie gives a few announcements. She invites the group to a meeting of Virgin Islands Writers' Association scheduled for the following week. She asks a woman named Veronica to talk about T-Shirts and the e-anthology. Veronica explains what the e-anthology is and says she will register everyone in the group. Valerie distributes a schedule and everyone takes note of the loggers, presenters and the composition of Reading and Writing groups. Valerie then invites the group to take a 10-min break.

It's a good time to escape from these people and find a more comfortable setting. I wiggle a little in the tight space, but couldn't see an escape route. Before long, the break time expires and my plan is thwarted. Valerie calls everyone to get ready to read the passion piece.

Passion piece? I wondered. What are these people so passionate about? I listen intently. I can hardly believe my ears. These people can truly write and read with a passion. They are so articulate!

A woman called Shamella wrote about her sons. In her writing she gives a riveting account of Elijah's journey. Ellen wants to know if every teacher has a philosophy of education. She takes the position that a quality education is the responsibility of the entire community. Michael takes time to explain the significance of his name, and Rhudel speaks about the importance of perseverance in his piece entitled "If I Could Do It." The verdant terrain of St. Lucia is captured in Merrencience's depiction of St. Helen of the West. Joyce's love for the color green leads her to share her piece called "The Color of My Passion." In her narrative about "A Yo-Yo Dieter," Luscilda describes her journey to lose weight and admitted that "individuality is better than outward conformity."

Ann's question "WHY?" is a reflection of the many ills plaguing our society, and she invites all to show more concern for others. Meritza's piece "Saturday Morning Blues" is captured in a short story. Meritza reminds all that the most important thing they would want to do in life is to be done with a passion." In her piece, Silvia addresses the issue of migrating to the Virgin Islands. She thanks God for opportunities to grow. Ruth decries the state of the island's roads in her poem called, "Paradise of Potholes, Beware." Carol speaks about the passion for her work, and expresses her commitment to ensure excellence at all times.

Charlene, a voracious reader, stresses the importance of reading as a gateway to life. Joan explains her passion in her piece called "Reflection." Natasha's reflection on, "The Death of Daddy's Little Girl" brings to life the struggles young people sometimes endure on their road to success. Nadia is "Driven for Success." She explains that "Competition" motivates her. Veronica states, "Life has run its course, but faith has brought the victory." Her piece entitled "Destiny" narrates the story of a young boy who overcame many difficulties to climb to the top of the ladder in his career choice. Valerie's "Passion for Mythology" is a vivid description of her students' research papers and their response to an assignment on mythology. Her presentation evokes periodic bursts laughter.

As if rewarding the writers for their efforts, the smell of freshly cooked food permeates the room. Lunch time brings cheers of excitement for the group as they proceed to have their meals. I was fooled into thinking that was all. But no! After lunch a woman named Sharon gathers the group and gives instructions on how to proceed in their writing groups. After an hour and 45 minutes, can you believe they have the nerves to return to the class when I was about to get my afternoon nap? Thank God the written pieces are not too lengthy this time. The groups share what transpired when they met. Meanwhile a group goes to the library to receive library cards. Written reflections summarize the day's activities.

Wow! What a day this has been! Although the people called themselves "writers," they were engaged in a variety of activities. Confident that everyone had left for the day, I dusted off my clothes and got ready to leave. Just then a young lady spots me on the floor. She quickly picks me up, turns me around and upside down.

"Whose pencil is this?" she questions.

Some look at me with disdain. I am so worn and tattered, that no one claims me.

"It's OK," I consoled myself. Today, I have seen, heard and done it all.

The lady walks to a box at the back of the room and places me in a box with my other friends. I didn't even know they were around. They, too, heard everything that was said about the importance of writing. It is only the first day of the Virgin Islands Writing Project Summer Institute. I can't wait to see what happens tomorrow!

A Second Look

By Joan Paulus

Surprising and life-giving initiatives can take place when we welcome the ideas of others into our usual way of seeing, thinking, and doing. During my nine-year tenure as a Language Arts teacher at the Positive Connections Alternative Education School, I was exposed to many opportunities for personal growth and enrichment by the very students we were designated to serve. Opening day was sometimes heart-wrenching with sobbing mothers who thanked the faculty repeatedly for accepting their children when "nobody else wanted them."

From its inception the school stressed the concept of "family" rather than "class." Students from junior high settings were sentenced there because of high risk behaviors such as lack of motivation, fighting, involved with drugs, and disrespect for authority figures; a few opted to be there because the school's location was closer to their home. The school's maximum capacity was seventy-five students. With only one school monitor, the faculty was petitioned to assist whenever an occasional dispute among students arose.

One day during the lunch period, I observed a commotion a short distance from my classroom. I called the monitor and headed in that direction. Two boys were struggling, so as I pushed closer to them I heard the words, "Get Paulus."

I suddenly was being lifted by two strong arms, one under my armpits and the other under my legs. "Put me down!" I demanded, and the tall male student gently rested my five-feet-one-inch frame down to the ground, in a standing position, away from the commotion. At that moment I started to laugh since I had never before been lifted by a student. As a matter of fact, everyone began to laugh, even the two boys who were struggling.

Upon further investigation, the boys explained that they were wrestling. It was a pastime they really enjoyed, challenging and testing each other's strength. With the assistance of the monitor and gym teacher, we submitted a proposal to the principal for lunch time wrestling when the students requested it. Those were fun moments for the faculty and student body, which resulted in fewer conflicts and more bonding and trusting. As for me, I still chuckle to myself whenever I remember that incident. It made me realize that no matter how hopeless a situation might seem, there is usually a tiny element of good to be found if we take time to look for it.

The Fisted Pebble: Teaching with an Open Heart and Hand

By Nancy Morgan

My posture was "straight as an arrow," as my Mom used to say, with shoulders back, arms lying flat at my side, curving at the elbow to reach behind my back. My three feet, one inch stature, still taller than the others, seemed to be embodied with authority. With fists pushed tightly together – one clutching a small pebble – I rocked a tiny bit forward, eyes squeezed shut as I pondered the question I would ask should the correct hand be chosen. My brother and sister were sitting on the bottom step. I didn't want them to run away, growing tired of the drama and the suspense. They never did. We were instructed to play, and the game had evolved a bit.

First, someone had to pick the correct hand. If chosen, then the question must be answered correctly, as well. I thrusted my fists forward, arms stretched out straight in front of me, opening my eyes simultaneously, to make certain that I was carefully balancing fists together so as not to give any advantage to the very perceptive siblings in front of me. My brother, four years younger than I, used to bend his neck to look under the knuckles, and my sister, two years older than he, seemed to want to ponder the trees first. I would sometimes look up, too, wondering if the answer had been reflected from my brain into the sky. It may have been a "tactic." Finally, someone would strike my fist with intention. It was the right hand! It could have been the left, however, and still be right! Wrong and right were confused with left and right at that point. Either way, the pebble was there, or not. Opening my eyes and smiling with the knowledge that though we'd all gotten the same information, they would not remember.

"What is the name of the President of the United States of America?" I asked, and looked deeply into their eyes one after another. The answer did not appear to be there. "Eisenhower," I said, tickled with delight, "Dwight D. Eisenhower!" It was an answer they should have known, because our Mom was working in his campaign, and she and Dad used to talk about it at the dinner table.

"How many states in the United States?" I would ask, as another of my favorite questions. I had repeatedly counted the 48 stars on the flag. I was thinking the answer could change, and who would know? I would ask mathematics questions, which my brother sometimes got correct. He would add using the buttons on his shirt if he had to, looking down and his fat little fingers fumbling up and down the front of the shirt, in order to arrive at an answer. He always knew that he wanted to be a physician and that mathematics was important for that reason. He even took trigonometry in high school! Impressive!

Soon, whenever we appeared on the front steps, a silent alarm seemed to be sounding. It was "game time!" We had the three children from across the street, cattycorner to the right the Reeds, and four of the six children from across the street, cattycorner to the left, the Williamses and on a rare occasion, Billy from next door. Usually, however, he just used to watch from across the fence, and when I glanced in his direction, he looked away, but every once in a while he would call out an answer, wait seconds for my nod or head shake no then disappear for a while. We knew it didn't count if he wasn't on the steps. He and I were a few months apart in age, but he was being raised by his grandparents and aunt and uncles so he knew a lot of grown-up things. At the time, I didn't mind his involvement, and he always seemed to surprise himself when he gave a correct answer. Sometimes he would be quietly watching from an upstairs window.

My little "mock" class, now competing for the teacher status that I enjoyed, could not ask me a question that I could not answer and could rarely answer the questions that I asked. I didn't know Bloom's taxonomy, but I did probe asking higher level thinking questions, especially when they looked as if they would get the obvious question right. They traditionally hovered around the bottom few steps unless we suspended the question part and relied solely on who picked the stone, but then, I always requested a question to be posed to me, and would end up on a top step again. Often I would be asked a question that I had asked, and no-one would know if my answer was correct or not. I would just smile knowingly.

The fundamental paradigm switch that occurred through those daily and weekly games, well before I went to formal school, was that I realized that asking the question was not giving the information, and that even saying the correct answer did not help the learner to digest and own the information. I could keep asking the same question every day but our toddler and pre-school Piagetian minds were not remembering isolated bits of information unrelated to a learning experience. I'm certain I knew all of this then, and if I'd had the vocabulary, I could have written this at the age of five and a half.

Actually, there are several themes that may surface as interests that have piqued my curiosity and captured my attention in the arena of education. The topics include emergent literacy, literacy across the curriculum, or reading and writing to learn; interdisciplinary or thematic teaching, assessment, and global education. Within each of the major topics there are undergirding assumptions that have to do with classroom management, differentiated instruction, peer interactions, play, special needs, relevant curriculum, standards, as well as correctly picking the hand with the pebble.

Even solitary play can contribute to the skills and strategies needed to speak, listen, write, or read. Observing a child playing with blocks may reveal a knowledge or propensity for identifying patterns, which are significantly found throughout language. Visual and auditory discrimination are pre-requisites to learning to read. In a brief video clip a child at the age of eight to ten months is pictured choosing blocks for a game of stacking them and laying them beside each other. He chooses carefully and places two blues and a yellow, then he places a red. He goes back to the original placements and adds a red in between and to the other end. This child was a reader by the age of three and a half years old identifying simple words and environmental print and reading at a fifth grade level by the age of five years.

Of course, there were many other language-related experiences involved, but identifying patterns putting puzzles together, and singing nursery songs with all of the words characterized him as unique in his age category, or maybe not. The fact that traditional tests of intelligence include patterns in problem-solving situations has some basis for credibility in observing developmental skills and tasks. Words, phrases, sentences, even texts, whether narrative or expository, are based on patterns. Speech has patterns, in any language. There may even be a pattern to picking the correct hand with the pebble in it, just as chance is studied in casinos by experts who have identified and have been alerted to certain patterns observed by the high-rolling winners and those who frequent certain games.

In several workshops and classes, I have asked people to write or talk about how they first learned to read. The most frequent answer is that a parent, a grandparent, a sibling, a specific relative, or a named teacher – later – sat with them and read to them and taught them the words and letters, and they could soon understand what was being read to them. In a few cases, there was a threat involved, which could be seen as the motivation that was needed at the time. Although few actually remember a specific time frame for learning to read, almost all can remember a person, a place, or a thing that catapulted them into the experience. In some cases, however, apparently the learning was more gradual. The meanings preceded the code and suddenly it all emerged.

It made sense through the constant exposure and related experiences. It appears that the awareness of learning to read happens in "retrospect." Therefore, perhaps any kinds of metacognitive skills that may be employed prior to the actual code-deciphering sequence are non-essential, or maybe not. Someone once said, "Once you know something, you cannot not know it." This is certainly true. But the question must be asked, "When do you know that you know?" Before teaching reading, all of us should ask ourselves the personal process question. Though in a college setting it would seem that all were readers, some still admitted that they were not certain of their reading ability. Almost all could, however, decode phonetically and could decipher print, though comprehension was not obviously admitted.

Reading for comprehension can be assessed through the use of an acronym used to remember the kinds of questions that characterize understanding material: FIVE. The F is for factual information. The reader will be asked something that appears in the text. The I is for inferential information. There is something that may be inferred from that which appears in the text. V is for vocabulary, which means that there is an understanding of terminology that appears in the text, or can be inferred from reading the text, and finally, the E is for experiential. The reader must be able to apply the information or infer or understand the relationship of the text to his or her life's experiences. The elements of whether or not someone understands what is being read can be found through this series of questions.

Teachers have found similar results when journaling and/or writing processes are followed, and the national trend to support writing development has been historically successful in enhancing student achievement through the National Writing Project. Years of success across the nation in promoting writing and the teaching of writing have resulted in funded programs and communities of writers and writing advocates. The movement embraces all and every discipline in grade levels pre-K to college. Writing and reading are simply processes, however, and are virtually ineffective without being viewed within the context of the content areas, or for the purpose of contributing to literature in my opinion. Others must agree. The Common Core State Standards have integrated language arts skills with content areas, further creating a more integrated curriculum that teachers and students can follow to successful learning experiences.

A practical example is evident in presentations prepared by classes I have taught for the past several years. A presentation on the potatoes included a book about a potato farmer for the area of literature; a geographical rendition of the places that potatoes are grown, including the discussion of the potato famine, which led to the growth cycle of the potato, and the uses and ways that they are used including to generate electricity. There was a game close to the "one potato, two potato" nursery rhyme, but also used the potato as having eyes that constituted seedling sprouts if given the life cycle changes or something like that. The point is, that each of the areas of social studies, science, mathematics, literature/English, the arts such as the making of Mr. and Mrs. Potato Head simulations and a dance that was taken from the nursery rhyme provided opportunities for interaction, action, and addressing what are referred to as Gardner's Multiple Intelligences. In addition, opportunities are created for both the right and left brain learners.

A rubric is developed by the class creating the criteria by which presentations will be assessed, and each student is made aware of the standard or expectations prior to the presentation. Peer evaluations are solicited, and in most cases except where there are obvious exclusions of met requirements, students have excelled. Each student must self-assess as well not just for the presentation, but also for all requirements of the course. The responsibility for learning is shifted to the learner, as in the locus of control model proposed by Rotter. The presentations must be research-based in terms of strategies and information conveyed. A performance-based portfolio is also required for all education courses I taught. The performance-based assessment is related to course instructional objectives.

During my lifetime the historical Berlin Wall was brought down; the Chernobyl disaster in 1986 pierced the Iron Curtain; the Wailing Wall of Israel is torn with bequests that vibrate daily across the world; and the Great Wall of China made up of human bits of frailty, and a little egg white are just a few symbols of our vulnerability in sitting on the steps. "Humpty Dumpty sat on a wall/ Humpty Dumpty had a great fall" is reminiscent of political satire in England in the nineteenth century.

Mom used to say that "if you hold your hand so tightly that nothing can get out, then nothing can get in." Our children are poised to preserve an economic and environmentally shared global space if we are aware of the challenges and the prospects for growth and development. What does this mean for our classrooms? What does this mean for our schools?

There are many distractions in the realm of education today. There are accusations of cheating on tests; there are acts of violence; there are issues of accountability and effective instruction, politics and monetary misuse. Further, it is easier to find one hundred famous athletes or entertainers than it is to hear about one hundred educators at the same media level of attention. Yet there are thousands and thousands of young people across the world who need to know some things. There are thousands of teachers who may or may not be revealing the pebble, and after asking the question, may not be willing to share the strategies necessary to succeed. Maybe like me they don't even know that the question is not the lesson. Maybe, in any different language the question is not the lesson.

Spirit Writing

By Mary Jo Wilder

For Ally "Chi-Gaumee-Kwe": daughter of Yale professor and great-great granddaughter of Anishinabe Chief John Boucher, my friend and confidant, spirit walker.

It was the end of July, months too late to be looking for a teaching job. I had just gotten up out of bed, to stand, on my own two feet for the 4th of July. A thyroid storm had knocked me out in March and lasted through four months of fevers, diagnosis and treatment. My daughters would drive the length and breadth of Michigan and back again and across three more states to get to Mayo for nuclear ablation. They were fearless that summer, planning two weddings and looking out for Mom. Had I not had two weddings to show up to, I would have checked out.

So it was; I awoke to find myself alive though weak and covered with Prednisone pearl like blemishes. Retirement funds were finished, but strangely, I was not. I needed money; I needed work. Serendipitously, there was an opening in my own backyard, a hundred miles from Marquette, where I was recovering and searching for work. "Yoopers" consider anything in the 350 mile stretch of Upper Peninsula their backyard. This is the wild northern frontier carved by the rocky Canadian Shield and Lake Superior to the north and Lake Michigan and Lake Huron to the south and snow, so much snow, nine months of the year.

Though the U.P. was clear cut in the 1800s, one would not know it for the tall pines lining the few main roads. It is home to bear, deer, moose, and wildcat. Little towns comprised of gas stations and post offices and perhaps a burger joint are sprinkled far and between the fill of a gas tank. One travels full with blankets, water and emergency supplies all year round as summer is short. All is green and blue or brown and white. This is God's country, Indian country. It has snowed in July.

Ironic that after spending too much on mailing complete job applications out of state, I would find an opening for an English teacher on the Bay Mills Indian Reservation some 25 miles outside of Sault Ste. Marie. I remembered the austere outpost. I had gone to the Casino once or twice to accompany friends spending their complimentary birthday tokens.

I called. Was this for real? I had paid too many $10 postage fees for packets to jobs that evaporated before the mail arrived. I was also leery of engaging yet again with another charter school, too many principals and directors with too little educational experience.

The principal answered the phone.

"Hello. I saw an online posting; do you have an opening for a middle school language arts teacher?"

He confirmed.

"Is this a living wage?"

He laughed, and I ended up faxing my resume.

Two weeks later I signed on with Mosaica, a **for** profit charter school company with home offices in San Francisco and Manhattan founded by a European couple with misty feelings about the name, Mosaica. I am leery of misty intentions. I would travel over the great bridge and some 450 miles south to be housed for a week of in-service training in a hotel near Detroit, and share smokes with a new co-worker at our tribal school. We would meet other young charter school recruits for the inner city schools. Our workshops covered crisis management and restraining holds. How had the Bay Mills Ojibwe Tribal Council become involved with this outfit?

I understood the need for a Native school at Bay Mills. Before the Casino was built, the road onto the rez had not been paved. I read that Native women, in the 20s, cleaned summer cottages for a pound of lard. In the 50s they sold their honey, berries, and wild rice to visitors. The community was limited and isolated as reserves were designed to be. Then the public school bus came as far as the reservation boundary, and kids were expected to walk, in all kinds of weather, three to five miles to their homes. This would be a feat for a well-fed athlete November through April. Why would one bother after a day of taunting or invisibility in the rural Brimley School? The white community this far north hadn't completely embraced multiculturalism then or now. So it was that the Ojibwe people were proud of the new portables with ten classrooms, a cafeteria and a few offices adjoining the community center.

I remember seeing my new simple cardboard-box-like school through the eyes of down state friends visiting me for a week. This building could not reflect the home offices of the mother company Mosaica in New York or California; there were building restrictions in high rent districts. Weren't there? The roof would have to be shoveled in winter, and the walls would leak in spring. My friends only asked, "Why Jo why?"

"Come with me; I'll show you." Then we drove and drove and drove along Lakeshore Drive, passing only an occasional car, past the lighthouse to Whitefish Bay, some 45 miles to the Pines, an uninhabited stretch of beach. We parked, and they ran down the needled path to Superior's edge, took in the ocean-like expanse, and the vanishing point off in the horizoned blue, the majesty, the splendor, the silence … the complete transport into the elements. Spirit world. After a long quiet spell, they shouted in the wind. We understand. We understand. This is good. Did they feel the sacred ground, ancient ground, site of the summer gatherings for the Ojibwe ancestors?

It would be the ancestors I called to every day during morning break, though this had never been my custom. I'd leave my classroom and the school second hour on my prep and drive right to Superior a few blocks over and sit on the beach offering tobacco, weeping, praying like I had never known how to before, and wondering what I had committed to, what I had done, how I could go on, how I could hold on to my health and benefits. When the calming came, I would return to my post and the rest of the day. Some days only three or four youth out of a dozen on the rolls would show up for my morning class. Some would simply put their heads down on the desks and sleep. Inevitably, someone would pass out on the floor. Some would ignore me and keep on with their chatting. Others glared. If a student needed the validation of a confrontation, the assistant principal would be called in. She was young and blonde, and the boys enjoyed playing her. On it went, weeks of glazed empty eyes, and tired weak bodies. To remember the dance of that time would be to extinguish my light. The mind simply shuts out what it cannot bear to see. It never happened. Somewhere in the first month, on my break by the water's edge, I discovered the library. I turned left.

Bay Mills Indian Community had a college! Just a few buildings really, but a college just the same, Michigan's first fully accredited, tribally controlled two-year college. My friend had been trying to tell me about it, but I was too far gone to hear her. Just off the road was a large attractive cabin-like structure maybe thirty feet across. I went in.

The mammoth log walls and open ceiling calmed the heart. Native arts, baskets, deer skin garments, beaded work, feathers, medicine wheels and a big dream catcher hung top to bottom and here and there. One felt at home. Half of the room was lined with books, shelving and a reading area. The other side housed rows of computers and a work station. I counted twenty in all. There it was, an aha moment. We could come here! Could we come here? We could do our writing homework (that never surfaced) in here. Maybe? I found the librarian and asked. I negotiated a field trip. I needed to check the students' reaction to the space and the technology. Most did not have computers at home; most would be technologically illiterate, but we could start. I needed to judge the distance and feasibility.

I remember walking into the Bay Mills Tribal School flanked by the ancestors in full regalia. In my head, the pow-wow singers were chanting, drumming, calling out. I found the Moasica administrator in his office where he always stayed, and I filled out the field trip paperwork for the first and last time. One can only wonder about moments where nothing and everything is right, and the universe opens up. I knew there would be no returned permission slips for youth where no one would be home to sign. Or if they could, I knew the Natives would not sign a document from a white man.

So it began as a field trip, a fast seven or slow ten minute walk from the portable school that would stretch across fall, winter, and spring. Seven minutes which would become an eye opening eternity in 5 below arctic clippers. We never asked again; we just left school when it was time for language arts. Most students showed up hatless and shoved ungloved hands in pockets. Several times, I witnessed a young man lend his coat to one of the girls in skimpy tees. The walk became a point of honor, seven minutes down the road, past the pond and cemetery. On the way we would greet the elders, discuss how we were, how our weekends went, what we wanted to write about. Always I offered a prompt, and always there was another option, and finally there was the sofa tucked back behind the reading nook where one could pass out and dream away all and any of life that had been too much. There were no behavior problems. We were awake. Was it the safe spot, the sacred art, or the fresh lakeside air that awakened us?

When it was really crazy weather, suddenly the bus driver would appear and ferry whoever wanted a lift though the young braves always walked, hatless or even coatless. It was a dance of honor.

However it was, they wrote, and I whispered, one-on-one like the Anishinabe, the original people. I retired my Jones New York work clothes for jeans and flannel shirts. I abandoned makeup. I crossed over. I had learned that everything about my early presentation was offensive: my look, my authority, my voice. I had been reared in urban wealth and upper middle class arrogance. The kids could smell me, and they were offended, challenged, and tuned out. Mine had been the historical language of violence. There was mistrust. We walked. We wrote. Wordlessly they handed me their words, and I corrected, and they rewrote, and I corrected and slowly the words became sentences, and the sentences became paragraphs, and we were ready for celebration. Sometime around that the community held the fall ceremony of thankfulness and harvest; we were ready, ready because we wanted to write about that. Our hearts were filling.

Once the recording was complete, after the last class of the day, I marched into the school with the four classes of English papers about the drumming, the singing, the Indian fry bread, the hull corn soup, the wild rice and the venison, the talking circle and the blessing, the gathering of the elders with the young. I started stapling those words to the walls throughout the school. I didn't care if the walls fell down. These were their words about their community, and I knew, knew like I have never had a knowing, that the words would carry, carry the unlawfulness of daily non-requisitioned field trips and unsanctioned library usage.

Then a thing happened that next morning as students and staff and teachers entered the building. Big small, old young started reading the walls. There was quiet. The bells rang. No one moved. Classes were late. There was pride. The bus driver came in to whisper, "You done good."

So it went; I learned to walk again that year, toe, heal. Aheeeeeee ... ah!

A Coach's Dilemma

By Rhudel James

How many of us have sat back in the comforts of our homes, watching an athletic event on TV and questioned every decision made by coaches? Those of us who have done this are called "arm chair coaches." With our family and friends, feasting on our favorite food and drink, we literally analyze, criticize, degrade, and demoralize the effort of coaches, despite their experience and success. Sometimes we applaud their skills.

We tend to be more critical of those individuals who willingly subject themselves to the scrutiny of being in positions of authority. When their teams are victorious, most of the credit goes to the play of the "gifted" athletes, the stars of the team. When the team loses, everyone knows, "it's always the coach's fault!"

Is doing this really fair, or does it simply come with the position? It is clearly not fair, and it does come with the position. In America, citizens have the right of "freedom of speech"; however, there are many cases where someone abuses that right. It truly does not matter what sport is discussed; the bottom line has always been victories versus losses.

What does it take for someone to be an athletic coach? How do you interpret coaching and what are the skills necessary to fulfill that role? What is gained by the person choosing to be a coach?

By definition, a coach is (academically) a private tutor; one who instructs or trains a performer or a team of performers; (athletically) one who instructs players in the fundamentals of a competitive sport and directs team strategy. To coach is to impart knowledge and skill, to discipline, educate, and teach.

Anyone desiring to become a successful coach should be prepared to expend a lot of energy, time and money, and experience the "thrill of victory and the agony of defeat."

It isn't a requirement for coaches to have played, at a high level, the sport which they coach. However, knowledge and experience of said sport are necessary in building a coach's credibility. Having the ability to convincingly manage a team with limited skills, resources, time and assistance, is highly desirable in coaching candidates.

Unfortunately, we all know of coaches who, in relation to the human factors involved, exhibit weaknesses in communication and management skills, and lack personal self-control. Somehow, they continue to coach despite their obvious challenges. We do question ourselves and friends about the true motivation of those who in our estimation, should stop confusing the minds of the young athlete and quit coaching forever. Bobby Knight, formerly of Indiana Hoosier fame, comes to mind; despite his genius for defensive strategies, he is a poor communicator. His passion is channeled through the use of fear and intimidation. "If he or anyone ever puts his hands on me, in an aggressive way, man I would … and end up losing my scholarship, my mind and my freedom!" said one potential recruit.

Personally, I have coached both academically and athletically and have had my struggles over the years. However, because of my love of competition, teaching and sports in particular, I have gained much insight into the deeper aspects of coaching. Many coaches are great in some areas, but in other areas, they stink.

I have chosen to coach basketball. Although I have had the privilege of coaching volleyball as well, basketball has always been my passion.

I began playing this sport because it came easily and it was fun. When I tried playing other sports, I didn't do very well. Due to my poor eyesight, I couldn't hit a softball or baseball to save my life; fielding wasn't any fun either. The game of cricket was never considered. I wasn't built for football and a practice or two proved that. I wasn't very big, fast or especially coordinated, so soccer was also out of the running.

Playing basketball was very different. I initially played without wearing glasses, but everything was blurred. With glasses, I began to excel at the little things at first. Eventually, my entire game came together.

I became a student of the game and could tell anyone everything about the history, players, statistics, and teams. As a player, I've had my memorable moments playing organized ball in high school and neighborhood leagues. Mainly a second string player in high school, I was a starter on the neighborhood teams. I even played a little in college, the military and church leagues as an adult. I had one major problem as a player; I was injury prone.

For whatever reason, I usually played with one injury after another. Bloody lips, cuts on the face, bruises, bumps and scrapes, torn knees and dislocated shoulders were a routine for me. This handicapping condition sidelined me for long periods of time, but led me to become a "bench coach." Having played for a number of coaches, with different styles and personalities, I took what experiences and strategies worked for me and shelved the rest. This also made me a better, smarter, defensive-minded player. Although capable of being a starter, in my opinion, I often got into the game to give the guy ahead of me a break, create havoc on defense, or as a decoy. My shot was pretty good too.

When I became a teacher and counselor the only other position I wanted was that of a coach. I waited for my dream to come true and believed that if given an opportunity, I could be the ultimate coach.

I seriously studied professional and college basketball teams, players and coaches. The coaches I found most impressive were big on communicating, nurturing and teaching: John Wooden (UCLA), John Thompson (Georgetown University), Dean Smith (North Carolina), Jerry Tarkanian (UNLV), Jim Valvano (NC State), NBA coaches Larry Brown, John Lucas II, Phil Jackson, Pat Riley and Lenny Wilkens, all now retired.

Many coaches, both former and present, including the ones mentioned here, have experienced the highs of success and the lows of failure. At one point or another, after winning seasons turned into losing ones, they accepted offers to coach other teams, resigned, retired or were fired. Only a chosen few remained with their teams on a long-term tenure.

Presently, I'm following the careers of the following current NBA coaches: Avery Johnson (New Jersey Nets), Byron Scott (Cleveland Cavaliers), Doc Rivers (Boston Celtics), Erik Spoelstra (Miami Heat), George Karl (Denver Nuggets), Greg Popovich (San Antonio Spurs), and Mike Woodson (New York Knicks).

I am in awe of the work of one college coach, Mike Krzyzewski, aka Coach K, (Duke). John Calipari and the Kentucky Wildcats featuring Player of the Year Anthony Davis is my choice to win the 2012 NCAA Championship against Bill Self and the Kansas Jayhawks with star forward Thomas Robinson. I also predict that Erik Spoelstra and the Miami Heat will be victorious over Scott Brooks and the Oklahoma City Thunder and win the NBA Championship in six exciting games.

My very first official opportunity to coach came when I was a high school teacher in Alachua, Florida, as a Boys' Assistant Basketball Coach at Sante Fe High School. My duties included academic monitoring, tutoring, teaching individual skills, running drills and keeping stats. I also ran scrimmages with the team. Being in a teaching mode, I didn't get hurt much because I learned how not to.

One memorable moment came at the end of an away game where my team was up two points with two seconds remaining to the end of regulation. The opposing team's point guard was about to shoot a three point shot, did so, but actually shot after the buzzer went off. The shot went in, but was waved off by the referees. A female parent came out of the stands and went after the referees who quickly retreated to the locker room. That was hilarious.

During that experience, I learned a great deal about the nuances of the game, the players, family and friends, as well as the secrets and strategies of principals and coaches. Some of the players went on to successful careers in college. That position lasted one year as I moved on to another assignment.

My next opportunity was when I was a counselor at an Alternative middle school in Charlotte, North Carolina. As the counselor in this school, my most important task was to motivate these students to stay out of trouble and stay in school. In assuming this challenge, I chose to use an athletic forum to communicate the importance of accepting personal responsibility and commitment to excellence in education.

For three years I was able to help some of these students transition from being "disruptive" to being "constructive." Practice was three hours long, intense and very competitive.

We competed against other middle schools and did very well. They trusted me and believed in my ability to teach, guide and nurture them into becoming more disciplined individuals. After three years, I was transferred to another Alternative program.

As a counselor in this second program for middle school students experiencing emotional and academic difficulties, I coached a team put together for the purpose of learning to work as one unit.

These students had been struggling in their regular schools and were at this alternative school for a second chance at attaining social and academic success. For two years we worked hard on academics and social skills building. We practiced three days a week and scrimmaged against much older guys. We only played against two schools; four games a year, but the lessons learned were priceless. I learned how to harness their athletic potential while focusing on academics and nurturing their growing maturity.

Decisions made by coaches to go one way or another have always been second guessed by those outside, and sometimes inside, the camps. In the game of basketball, it seems that everyone and his/her dogs have opinions as to what a coach should or should not have done.

Just recently, another one of my favorite coaches, Nate McMillan, was relieved of his duties with the Portland Trailblazers for reasons I know were beyond his control. Unlike the Knicks' recently replaced coach, Mike D'Antoni who had basically lost his players' confidence, McMillan was well respected and trusted by his players.

It really didn't matter that both are also coaches of Team USA with Coach K; their time was up.

If ever I had a losing season like most coaches with losing seasons, being fired would be the logical result; this season was it. I am not ashamed that I haven't coached on the college or professional level. Having the chance to coach at the high school and middle school level, I take my responsibility seriously. Influencing the minds and characters of the younger players is a once in a lifetime opportunity.

The challenge I faced daily was managing the mix of personalities, raw talent and character of the players with very limited resources.

This year, my fourth at Elena Christian Junior High in St. Croix, USVI, after three moderately successful campaigns, was exceptionally tough.

About 25 eager candidates tried out for the team and I selected 20 for the active team (15) and a practice team (5). Students at this age group (12 -16) are somewhat emotional and immature and it wouldn't have taken much rejection to deflate their egos. Knowing the tentativeness of the middle school temperament, I anticipated the need for additional players. I enlightened the chosen ones about the probability that some of them would not make it through the shortened, six-game, season. The possibility of poor academics, poor attitudes and poor luck with injuries could become a problem. I emphasized the importance of conditioning, effort, following instructions, leadership, listening and patience. I preached about character, citizenship, commitment and creativity. I focused on the team concept.

We could use 15 players in tournaments, but only 12 during the season. With only 6 games for the season, tournament games gave the players an opportunity to demonstrate their skills. Before the season began I decided we would play against the older, bigger boys, junior varsity aged 15-16, and not the middle school aged boys 12-14.

This decision was based on past success and the belief that producing the greatest growth in youth is a result of playing the stiffest competition. My team was perhaps the smallest when compared to the others, but I believed we could hold our own and win games if we played up to our potential. The skill level of this team was low and suggested we had a lot of work.

Practice was held for two hours, four days a week. I encouraged the players to work on their individual skills over the weekend. I challenged them to become students of the game and gave them trivia research assignments identifying NBA coaches, players and teams. I questioned them spontaneously before, during and after practices.

There are coaches who are identified by their penchant for defense or offense, for being tough or demanding, for being motivators. There are those who would do almost anything to win; their motto being "Winning is everything!" There are those of us who are teachers at all times and talk a little too much (according to some players). Then there are those of us who couldn't care less what anyone thinks and run our teams exactly the way we want to.

There are those who put athletics ahead of academics and pay a high price for winning (and losing), often at the expense of their players, schools and reputations. Is it possible that the 2011-2012 Syracuse University Men's Basketball team became a casualty of this viewpoint? Did the legendary coach Jim Boeheim have anything to do with his star center, 7'0" 255 lbs. Fabrico Paulino de Melo (Fab Melo) being ruled ineligible for the NCAA Tournament? Could he be responsible for Melo's academic struggles? Was it the coach's fault that his team lost its number one standing and lost before it got to the Final Four?

Did the coach value athletics over academics and used Melo, despite his apparent academic difficulties? I am very sure there are plenty people who believe this coach is guilty and to be blamed for the Orangemen's fall from contention. I can relate to being unfairly blamed.

I am a nurturing coach, the challenging, counseling, drilling, motivating, repetition, teaching type. I expect my players to also develop a deeper understanding of the fundamentals, specifics and nuances of the game. As I lead by example, I expect my players to learn from their mistakes.

I expect them to play better, harder, smarter from game to game. I expect my players to buy into my philosophy of "games are won 75 percent of the time by team play, 15 percent individual effort and 10 percent luck." In my estimation, some team strategy enables a team to score 75% of the time. Twenty-five percent of the time a team scores because of one or more individuals exhibiting exceptional effort. Without explanation, plain old luck accounts for "bail-out" points—the toss ups we never expected to go into the basket, but relieved that they did.

Sometimes, a player's ability to anticipate and take advantage of the opposing team's tendencies, weaknesses and mistakes turns into fast break points. The players' basketball IQ becomes evident in their play. The individual player's skill level often leads to baskets (3 of 5 times) because he has learned to read the other team's offensive sets and has begun to show leadership in his communicating this information with teammates. Most coaches dictate offensive and defensive schemes and try to explain everything possible to their players, leaving nothing to chance.

Sometimes, God smiles on teams and allows his angels to get into the games with assists. The acrobatic shots made in this game are simply incredible.

When reality sets in, my warnings come true. In addition to my team's immaturity and lack of self-discipline, commitment to practice was non-existent. This group's ability to listen and execute as directed was a struggle from the beginning. They were, in effect, intimidated and I did not do a good job in helping them to overcome this obstacle.

This caused me to second guess my decision to play JV instead of the younger, smaller middle school teams. Perhaps I overestimated the potential of this group.

Having access to my team's grades, I had no choice but to follow through on my warnings about what would happen when prioritizing academics above athletics was not followed. Nine of my twelve players became casualties of "the unexpected" as the team suffered from an unanticipated meltdown. Two players were lost temporarily because of injury, four were cut due to academic failures, two were cut by their parents also because of poor grades, and one was cut due to persistent disrespect.

While the two injured players returned (not at full strength) along with two of seven originally cut (Principal's decision), the starting five now had three new members. In effect, the team's chemistry was negatively affected by replacement players. The skill level of the team was significantly lowered, but the energy of this "new" team rose.

I am also guilty of making some questionable decisions, taking chances and challenging my players to do more than they might have been capable of. These decisions weren't easy ones and there was some bad luck with the injuries. Still these circumstances contributed greatly to our 0-6 demise (one game was forfeited for academic reasons); my very first season without a win.

What is a coach to do when pressure to win comes from everywhere? What guides the conscience of an experienced coach who has to make decisions that sometimes hang career and players' egos in the balance?

I simply treat players with respect, challenge them to do what it takes to get better every day, study the game, make decisions using common sense and learn from my mistakes.

Every coach looks for a silver lining in spite of disappointments. I hope that my players understood the significance of the decisions I made both on and off the court. I hope they realized that there's no 'I' in team. A team is only as good as its leadership and confidence in its players.

I hope that as they continue on with their athletic activities, they come to understand that without practice, nothing becomes perfect. Hard work equals success. I hope, in time, they appreciate how they were nurtured and spoken to with respect. I hope they become better players, better students and better people.

Among all that I learned this year, one thing about motivating this age group stood out. Despite my chiding, encouragement and pleadings for quality effort during practice and in games, the offer of a pizza party at season's end proved more motivating than anything else. I too, am looking forward to that party.

These ponderings of this coach's dilemma are dedicated to the memory of a very dear friend, a colleague, fellow coach and mother of four young children, Miss Nefertiti O'Bryan. Thank you for your spirit.

Your energy, enthusiasm, and devotion to your family, students and athletes at Elena Christian Junior High School can never be duplicated. Watching you coach basketball, pacing up and down along the bench with your children in tow, inspired me to return to the sidelines. You will never be forgotten.

Update: I was correct in picking the Kentucky Wildcats to win the 2012 NCAA Championship, the Miami Heat to win the 2012 NBA Championship and the Baltimore Ravens to win the 2013 Super Bowl. Coach Mike D'Antoni has been hired to coach the LA Lakers; wrong choice in my opinion. I was also transferred to another school at the end of the school year. Was this coincidence or conspiracy?

Supporting Students for Literacy Success

By Sharon Charles

When one considers the diversity that exists among students in today's classroom, it is quick to realize that the task of helping students to become more effective writers can present a challenge even to the veteran teacher. The classroom teacher has to be prepared for this challenge if he/she is expected to see significant gains in students' writing. Evidently writing is hard work. It takes time and practice if students are to be good at it.

There are several useful strategies that teachers can use to help students gain proficiency in writing. I believe that writing teachers should be writers themselves. For this reason, teachers should model the type of writing they want students to do. Also, to gain support for writing in the classroom, teachers should write with their students. This not only sets the tone for writing and emphasizes its importance, but it gives students the confidence to develop their own writing.

Teachers have the capability to provide an atmosphere where students can support each other. Peer tutoring, writing workshops, individual conferences and writing response groups can go a long way in providing support for students. Teachers should always encourage students to think of the purpose for their writing and the audience for which the piece is written. In addition, students should also be given opportunities to writing in different genres. If classroom teachers give students the tools to write, and provide them with time to adequately practice, this will help them to gain the skills that will need to make them more proficient writers.

Dough Boy

By Valerie Combie

There he goes, a chubby little body with fat cheeks bulging over his lips. His short stubby legs shake as his Reebok-clad feet take him forward from the parking lot to his third grade classroom. His right hand pulls a bulging backpack on wheels laden with his books, while in his right hand he carries his lunch box. On his back is another backpack, which contains his PE uniform, as well as additional books and his recorder. He is a dedicated student, highly competitive, determined to complete the school year with the highest grade.

Each assignment has been completed to his parents' satisfaction; Spanish and French vocabulary and verb conjugations have been studied; not only has he practiced the recorder, but he completed his mandatory hour of practicing the piano. He enters his class and deposits the contents of his roller back pack on his desk. He arranges the books according to the day's schedule, with the books for the first class on top, continuing to the last class of the day. He then places his lunch box on the shelf built on the southern wall of the room and places the back pack with his PE uniform on the bottom shelf. From the backpack, he takes two books, pushes his chair under his desk, and exits the room. He walks hurriedly down the corridor, passes the fourth grade classroom, turns right, where he greets Mr. R. the school's business manager, with a cheerful smile. He hops down the steps, walks briskly down the hedged and paved walkway.

The school buses are depositing their human cargo just as walks under the grape tree. He greets the teacher on bus duty as someone shouts: "Hey, guys, here comes Dough Boy! Did you feel the earth shake?"

Loud laughter issues from the yellow school bus as other voices shout: "Hoo, Hoo! Pillsbury Dough Boy!"

He ducks under the branches of the grape tree, chubby cheeks ballooning and lips pursed, but there's a determined look in his brown eyes as he tries to escape the jeering sounds of laughter and loud voices. He continues on the paved walkway and enters the library where the librarian greets him affectionately: "Good morning, little reader, what have we today?"

The sadness disappears and a smile replaces the pursed lips. "I have read three books, Mrs. Mault, and I'm going to take out another *Amelia Bedelia* and *Pippi Longstocking.* Aren't those girls funny?"

"They sure are, Sweetie. You know where they are; you can check them out and take a new book mark."

"Thanks, Mrs. Mault."

He drops his books in the RETURNING BOOKS bin and turns to the Children's Fiction. He stops momentarily and addresses the librarian. "Mrs. Mault, do you know what's my greatest wish?" Before she could answer, he continues. "I wish I could stay in the library, lie on my favorite rug, with my favorite cushions around me, and read all my favorite books."

"I can understand not being interrupted by having to go to classes, but won't you want to break for lunch?" Mrs. Mault asks.

"Well, yes. I'd break for lunch," he concedes, then he rushes over to the Children' Fiction as some classmates push the library door open and enter. He heads straight for his target, collects his books, goes over to the reading corner, snuggles up on the rug, with the cushions at his back, and starts to read.

The first bell rings, warning him that he has ten minutes to get to class. He jumps up, replaces the cushions, takes his books to the circulation desk where he checks the stamp for the correct date, stamps the books, and writes his name on the line. He grabs a book mark and runs out of the library, shouting a speedy "Bye, Mrs. Mault!"

He runs past groups of students as he retraces his footsteps to his classroom. The teacher welcomes him at the door, and he puts his books in his back pack, reshelves it, and sits attentively at his desk. He is at peace in this room. His peers may taunt him on the playground or on the spacious campus, but in the classroom, he is too busy learning and so are they, too busy to call anyone names or to bully any one. This teacher does not allow such disrespectful behavior.

For PE, the class is swimming. He dons his huge swim trunks, walks in line with his classmates and stands at the edge of the pool. At the coach's command, each student jumps into the water and swims three laps. He loves swimming, and he's a good swimmer. It's his turn and he jumps into the pool and executes his three laps, too intent on swimming to hear the loud laughter and unkind remarks of his classmates: "Duck, Dough Boy has caused a tsunami! It's Dough Boy! It's a baby whale! See how the water rises!"

He completes his laps and climbs out of the pool as his coach pats his shoulder and says: "Good job. Hit the shower."

The scenario is repeated each day, but he continues his routine, studying diligently, ignoring the taunts that hurt so much because he knows that his parents love him; he's his grandparents' treasure; his other relatives and all adults love him. He feels sorry for the students who taunt him, but when they ask him to help with assignments, he does so patiently and willingly.

He completes each grade with honors, twice representing his school in the Spelling Bee; once representing the Territory in the Conde Nast My Caribbean Essay Contest. And the Dough Boy taunts continue. During Middle School, he starts to lose weight and by his eighth grade promotion, he has lost forty pounds! The Dough Boy has lost his dough. The taunts change, but he continues to pursue his goal, reading voraciously and imbibing knowledge. During the difficult stages when he experiences problems with calculus, he seeks out the teacher for extra help after school. He plays the trumpet in the school band, but he continues learning and practicing the piano.

He attends the Junior Statesman Program at Yale University and the University of Maryland. He becomes an AP scholar, graduates as the class valedictorian, and receives a scholarship for college.

The Dough Boy pumps iron, runs miles, exercises religiously, and eats healthily. He maintains his weight and jokingly looks at his elementary school pictures and claims: "I love those chubby cheeks! I sure miss Dough Boy!"

Confessions of A High School Marketing Teacher … I'm An Artist

By Stefanie Samuel

"There is no more noble profession than teaching. A great teacher is a great artist, but his/her medium is not canvas, but the human soul" ~ Anonymous

Reflection:

As a teacher with an artistic flair, my paint brush comes alive in my classroom. I stroke yellow shades on students who are blue and calm greens on students who are red hot. I use humor to add splashes of color. There is no time to sleep when creativity is brewing. Disrespectful students are pulled out of the palette until their canvases are cleared. Rule breakers pay $1.00 fee, which makes them green. This contributes to the "A" students white smiles. Sleep during instruction is rare but not tolerated; with a few strokes of my brush I awake energy and vivid imagination. As an artist, I am constantly in search of my inspiration to use in the classroom that encourages students to find their inner masterpieces. My favorite quote from one of my masterpieces is "Wha! Class finish already?!" when the bell rings.

My work here is done.

A Story to Tell

By Mary Jo Wilder

The 99.5 radio broadcaster announces at every break about the up-and-coming cultural extravaganza "Story Toh Tell" at Fort Frederik on October 1st. Hearing this message every day for three weeks, during my commute to and from the university, I am convinced. My uninspired writing class is going. Friday's class will meet Saturday at the fort for inspiration.

I suppose this class outing is self-serving; I can walk. I round the corner from my apartment at Liberty Hall in Frederiksted and take in the ribbon of ocean blue four blocks away. Massive walls of coral, molasses and mortar, ruins and refurbished great houses, line Hill Street down, and across Prince, Queen, King, and finally Strand Street to the waterfront walkway. I desperately want my students to value the layers of history here on their island. Do they realize it was their ancestors that carried the knowledge to build these stone arches for the colonial masters? Turning north towards the fort I am startled from my reverie. Two cruise ships are in; the city block next to the pier is cordoned off for a string of white tents and vendors. Quelbe and Calypso beckon tourists and locals alike. People are everywhere. A real crowd. Town is a buzz. What a nice coincidence!

I spot about a dozen students under the trees by the gazebo in Budhoe Park. "Ms. Wilder, we didn't know you with that hat. You look like a tourist!"

I smile, "Good morning! I needed some protection. Let's wait a few more minutes, and then we'll go in."

We chat a while; they inform me others are coming. Years of living and working here, I know not to wait, but to move on when we get a critical mass. A few more join us, and I motion for us to move towards the entrance of the fort. I remember reading that it was constructed in the 1750s "to protect the town from pirate raids and attacks from rival imperialist nations." I chuckle thinking about pirates. From the end of the pier, the fort looks like a red, two tiered Christmas cake, skirted by a sea wall with a dozen cannons.

To our surprise, we are welcomed, registered, and handed programs by a guide from the Virgin Islands Humanities Council. My, my, I had no idea. The coordinator of the event comes up to me and invites us to the breakfast inside. Second lovely coincidence! I have hungry young men with me.

We enter, and I huddle the group inside the stone courtyard, and I extend the invitation for food after we finish our research. I encourage everyone to visit at least three displays while the cooks are setting up. We spread out, some to the turn of the century photos from Frenchtown while others move off to the slave exhibition, the officers' quarters, and the dungeon.

Women in brightly colored yellow and orange traditional madras skirts and kerchiefs staff the sale tables. Miniature Mock-o-Jumbies whirl from wooden sticks alongside baskets, gourd instruments, local crafts, books and CDs. Musicians, tourists, travelers, and presenters begin to fill the courtyard. We are in a state of wonderment, a magical mystery tour that none of us imagined. We are "feelin' it" happy, happy, happy: local history, local vendors, local music. I can't wait to read their writing.

A week later the essays come in.

"Me son, me no no were wees goin til wees see she in da park with dat hat."

I am angry, frustrated and overwhelmed!

By the seventieth some essay, I am beginning to wonder why … What possessed me to insist on a field trip for developmental college writing? Where is the food tent with rows of linen covered tables holding silver warming dishes and delectable food platters catered by our five star hotel?

Magically, I thought what? I thought an outing could cure culturally insensitive textbooks, an island held under seven different flags, seven different nations, languages and cultures. It seems a cruel twist of fate that my students must write in English when their tongues have been encoded for West African sounds. And … Cruzan is its own language!

Spent, I reluctantly pull up the last paper and read, "What was Ms. Wilder thinking? It was Saturday, and I had things to do, but I needed to pass this class and complete the assignment. Funny thing is, it turned out to be the best day of my life!"

"Oh Lord," I thought. Then Adisha explains, that while writing her field notes in the Commandant's Quarter's on the second floor of the old fort, she looked up to catch a young man staring at her. The glance was electrifying. She wrote that she dropped all of her things, and the next thing, Prince Charming was at her side assisting her in picking up the paper mess. They both laughed and went on their ways. What? I read it again.

Adisha seems a few years older than the other eighteen-year-olds in the class. She is attractive, not just perky pretty, but a full woman in all of her bearing. It seems she has fought her way back to college, delayed by something, and hungry to learn, so their conspiratorial laughter and wisdom, the prince-stranger and the student, make sense. She continues exploring the other rooms, displays and grounds noting details, but clearly charged by the exchange. I read on.

The next week, I am full up with more days of grading and not particularly happy when I walk into my four o'clock writing class.

"Class listen. I am both disgusted and thrilled, distraught and encouraged."

I throw the corrected essays down on the table. "I am angry that either you were not taught, or you do not care to write complete sentences or coherent paragraphs. If you did not learn in your twelve years of school, I am simply angry, angry, angry at the local schools. However, whatever the case, we are all adults here. I need you to dial it up. I need you to own your education right now. The alternative is bagging for Plaza. Tomorrow is the midterm. The essay question comes from the English Department. We will write a narrative essay." On I go linking the midterm essay question to all we have covered in the last eight weeks.

"What I have not taught you is how to write an implied thesis. I haven't taught you that because it is the easiest and the hardest to write. I have demanded you write an explicit thesis because I want to know what you are going to tell me, and I want you to know what you have committed to saying. In a way, you need to write an explicit thesis for this narrative and then go back and write the same thing in an implied way."

I look out at the class. It is only 4:15 and already their eyes are clouding over. They are tuning out.

Let me give you an example. One of your classmates in my morning session went to the fort on Saturday, and it was the best day of her life. That's her thesis. Is it implied or explicit? I tell them about Adisha, about how she was making notes in the officer's quarters when zh-hzzzzz------- she looked up to see the man of her dreams staring at her. The class looks up. I have their attention. Adisha was so shaken that everything fell from her arms. He rushed to help her. She's a little older, I explained. They both laughed at the silliness of the situation.

Then, she went about her business. I couldn't resist saying, in a loud voice, "She filled out all of her pre-writing sheets as she proceeded through the various exhibits."

I continue, "Outside of the fort by the gazebo, she collected herself. I guess she looked out and took in the cruise ship. There, standing on the wharf was her prince. Their eyes locked on. They both laughed. Finally he came over and introduced himself. He explained he was on the cruise and pulling out in a few hours. Apparently he said, 'At least let me have your number.'"

One of the students shouts out, "It's just like a fairy tale!"

Everyone is smiling and feeling good.

"Now, what Adisha wrote was a narrative. You've been hearing it your whole life, so don't be threatened by your mid-term question. However, for obvious reasons the implied thesis sometimes is better than an explicit one. If Adisha had written, I didn't want to go to the event in Frederiksted, but I did, and saw the man of my dreams, and dropped my things, and he came to my rescue, and we exchanged numbers it wouldn't have been as interesting. That would be like someone asking you for a date and telling you he expects a kiss before the night is over. That could be just icky. Maybe he wants the kiss, but the explicitness just ruins it."

"Ok, Ms Wilder, then what happened?"

"I'll tell you, but first you need to hear this. You too have stories to tell. Connect with what's all around you, and what is in here. I put my hand on my heart for drama's sake. Adisha did!"

They are impatient now.

"Ok, later that night, when he was out at sea, he called," I pause. "They talked till morning."

The eyes are wide.

"Yup. He lives in Atlanta. She was already planning to move there this January before this happened."

There is silence. We are sitting with our goose bumps. We are sitting with wonderment. I reflect on the times men have fallen out of the sky for my daughters and me.

One of the males pipes up, "That was an interesting coincidence."

"Nope," I say, "I don't believe in accidents."

The students gather up their books, and reorders the room from our workshop configuration. Our mood is lighter. We are united in the warmth of possibility.

We head out down the hall and through the double doors together, and there is "coincidentally," Adisha, my essay writer, in her cool gray and pink turbaned head scarf talking vibrantly on her cell. She looks at me and then points to the phone in a very theatrical gesture. I turn to my students that have escorted me out, "That is Atlanta calling now." They get it. Suddenly, we are all quite giddy. We do celebrate good stories in the islands.

That Day at Gardenville

By Veronica Prescott

The sky was overcast and the smell of rain filled the air. I was reluctant to leave home. I entered my car wondering what that day at Gardenville Elementary was going to be like. I arrived ten minutes late. By then, the torrential showers were pounding on the campus grounds, forcing water into every crevice. The bell rang, nonetheless, signaling the commencement of another instructional day.

Students were scampering to their classrooms: some ducking guttering overflows, others were sprinting over puddles to avoid getting wet. Teachers and para-educators were hustling to the office, determined to beat the punch-clock on the wall. Canopied by their umbrellas, their varied attires displayed an array of colors: black, red, blue, green, pink, maroon, and others.

I, too, joined the fray as I scurried through the crowd, fighting to evade the heavy downpour. I had to stop on occasions lest I tripped on one of those puny students as I stepped on to the balcony. I was being stopped repeatedly to get hugs and recognizable "Good mornings" as students made their way to class.

My heart is always delighted when I see smiles on the faces of our students. I envision an attentive classroom with some intelligent minds ready to absorb the instruction for the day. On the other-hand, I wonder about the minority who seldom smile, attending class unkempt and most times, on empty stomachs. I empathize with those little ones who are left to walk to school unsupervised. Who cares for these unfortunate children? Who is there to give a "goodbye" hug-and-kiss as they set out for their day? Who says, "I love you, and have a good day in school"? Who peruses their homework assignments to ensure that they are done correctly? Who plays the role of guardian angel?

My reverie was interrupted that day by the familiar knocking and the anxious voices outside my classroom door. I leapt out of my chair with many questions crowding my mind. "What a day am I having today? It is raining on the outside. Is there going to be thunder and lightning on the inside? What other technique can I use? I need something appropriate! I need some positive results today, and I want today to be different especially for J.B.," I thought to myself.

I moved cautiously towards the door. With my hand on the doorknob, a deep sigh, I prayed softly: "Lord, give me new strength and courage for today. Help me not just to tolerate these students, but to make a difference." With that said, I opened the door and in rushed a swarm of bees, pushing and shoving each other. I silently watched as they entered and dropped into their seats.

"Let's do that one more time!" I demanded. All eyes stared in my direction puzzled. "We are going to go out of the door, and walk back in the proper way," I emphatically ordered.

As they calmly reentered the room, one by one they echoed, "Good Morning, Ms. Prescott."

"Good Morning boys and girls," I replied. "And how are you doing today?"

"Fine" they chimed in unison.

"Today, we are going to do some real fun reading on the computer."

"Yea!" someone shouted from the corner.

"Can we play games?" another asked.

"Not until you hear this story," was my response.

The story of "The Three Little Pigs" projected on the Promethean Board attracted much attention.

"Look, the three little pigs!" Came the soft spoken voice from the middle of the class.

"The wolf is going to eat them!" Shouted another.

As the story unfolded on the screen, not a sound could be heard except the clattering of the two units placed on either corner of the room. I looked around in total bewilderment wondering what had happened to my raucous class. Where was the class which predetermined how I should spend my day? Where are the talkative students who kept me so busy for the first forty-five minutes?

I scanned the room briefly wondering what had come over them. They were all sitting quietly with eyes glued to the promethean board absorbing every bit of information about the story.

Finally, I was able to put the final piece to the puzzle. Although the torrential rain showers continued to pound on the outside, it was like sunshine in my classroom. The time sped by quickly. The students were disappointed they did not get to see the end of the story. It was to be continued the following day.

As they stood in line to march back to their class, a sudden calmness came over me, and I smiled. I checked my attendance book. J.B. was the only one absent that day!

As the teacher of a computer lab, my day begins with Kindergarten and ends with Third Grade!

Getting Through

By Rhudel A. James

I had been thinking of what my reaction would be if one day my class rejected my challenges and openly rebelled against me. Initially, I thought, this would never happen. I was wrong.

The day started normally with me ushering my students into the classroom. After getting them settled, I announced that there would be a pop quiz, based on last week's discussion, instead of the usual bell work. I challenged them, as always, to think outside the norm, to be creative and to give me their best. As a matter of fact, I demanded their best. They were to write an essay on decision making, incorporating the points made in last week's discussion.

To my amazement, they sat there and did nothing; looking at me as though I'd just given them the worst news; they all appeared to be in shock. Why weren't they doing what I asked? I repeated my instructions, but they just sat there, silently, staring at me blankly, without emotion or expression.

I was at a loss for words; I didn't know what to do. Attempting to save face and not appear as though I'd lost control of the class, I sat down and became silent as they were, trying to figure out what was happening. What were they thinking? Would I have to get the principal or the monitors to assist me? I had no choice but to wait on their next move. These thoughts, filled with fear and anxiety, went on for an inordinate amount of time, five very long minutes.

I couldn't take the suspense anymore and finally broke the silence by questioning a student with whom I had a good rapport. He remained mum. Without warning they all burst out laughing. I was confused. Then to my rescue came the class clown.

"Coach, remember what we discussed last week? We talked about thinking outside the box and presenting ideas beyond the moment. Well, we decided as a group, to put you to the test. We were protesting silently, being passive aggressive; allowing you to go crazy with your thoughts. Once we explained what we were doing, we would then write about our thoughts and the experiment. What do you think, Coach?"

I was humbled. I had gotten through to them and didn't realize it. I was truly relieved that they weren't going to revolt and we wouldn't be on the evening news or on the front page of the local paper. They had made their point. They had become the teachers and I had become the student.

A Whole New World

By Abigail Martyr

Joana was not like other little children. In a world where children were preoccupied with television sets and video games, Joana would much rather have opened a book. It was a rather strange sight to see anyone with a book, much less a child. But then if you had her abilities, you would want to read all the time too.

Joana discovered her gift at the tender age of five. Her grandmother had given her the book *Cinderella* as a birthday present. You see, Grandma shared Joana's gift, and in her wisdom realized that the gift must be cultivated early. Initially, Joana was not very happy with her birthday present—she would have preferred a game for her brand new Nintendo DS, to be perfectly honest. But when she opened the book and started reading, the most amazing thing happened.

Her room was immediately transformed. It was as if the book had come to life right there in her room. She saw the ivy-covered house that Cinderella lived in with the beautiful hedges and flowering gardens. She cried at seeing the terrible treatment Cinderella received from the hands of her wicked stepmother and stepsisters. Joana was also seated in the very first row at Cinderella's wedding when she married the Prince. That was the best scene of all.

When Joana finished reading *Cinderella*, she was eager to see if the same thing would happen with a different book. She immediately ran to Grandma who was expecting to see Joana at any moment. "Are you looking for this?" Grandma asked with a knowing smile as she handed Joana the book *Thumbelina*. Joana quickly took the book back to her room and was amazed when it, too, came to life before her eyes. Since then, Joana and Grandma have shared many adventures in the pages of the books that they read. Sometimes they even write stories of their own. They enter a whole new world every time they read.

It may be hard to believe, but you too have Joana's gift. It may have been dulled by watching too much TV and other distractions, but with practice it can be sharpened no matter your age. Open a book and read, or pick up a pen and write. Your adventures are limited only by your imagination.

My Compatriots

By Christopher Combie

Over the past two years, I have had the opportunity to work with and teach a diverse group of students from within the United States to the islands of the West Indies and countries in Central America. My two stories express my interactions with students who would have been considered unreachable.

The first two young men share several factors in common with me, and I remember the first response I received from them after welcoming them into our graduate program. The response sent was rather unprofessional based on our relationship, but the gist of the message was an invitation for me to "chill with them" and their fraternity brothers. Dissecting the email response and reading between the lines, I thought, "Do they know the commitment that is required in this graduate program, and are they ready for the challenge?" Needless to say, I prayed that God would guide me in my interactions with them and that He would use me to role model for them to be successful in academe and beyond.

During the orientation to the graduate program in the fall, I presented a writing workshop to prepare the incoming cohort for the rigors of academic writing at the graduate level. After the presentation, the two men approached me and confessed that their writing skills were weak, but that they were willing to put in the effort to enhance their skills. I committed to helping them along the writing continuum and provided them with additional resources, such as our Writing Center, and peer mentors to help with proofreading. During the spring semester, I taught both men in a traditional class and I pored over their papers in an effort to provide them with tangible feedback to advance on the writing continuum. The men did not receive high grades and had to rewrite a few papers and make additional trips to the Writing Center, but I know they learned a great deal in the process.

How, you might ask? I noticed a few things: the men became more self-confident in their formal and impromptu presentations in the classroom; their deportment in responding to in-class discussions greatly improved; and the note I received at the end of the semester from them indicated as such. Although the men earned grades to pass the course, they were not grades that I would have deemed acceptable on my report card. Nevertheless, they wrote me notes of appreciation at the end of the semester thanking me for my patience in helping them to enhance their writing skills and for my willingness to care.

You see, many of the faculty at my institution are not accustomed to dealing with so called "problem students" for which one must really hone in on learning style and actually teach so students can understand. Rather than simply dismiss them and shuffle them off to another office as is the norm at my institution, I treated them as persons first and as students second. (I guess it stems from my training as a clinician and therapist whose instructors always drilled "person first, symptomology second.") One of the beauties of the program in which I teach is that the faculty treat students as family and consider the students' holistic development (academic, personal, physical, intellectual, spiritual, etc.) in all their interactions. Whereas many faculty members are only concerned about the assignments due and the students' satisfactory progress, our faculty approach delves deeper.

The other student is from Central America and English is not his first language. He was placed on a probationary status after his first semester within the program. I was not surprised, nor was he. Why? You might ask. I remember his admissions' interview when I sat with him and the panel of the admissions committee and the question was asked how he would transition to graduate school after having served as a president of a student organization as an undergraduate at the same institution and being *supercool* involving himself in every aspect of the undergraduate student experience. He solemnly swore that he would recuse himself in order to focus on the demands of his graduate program.

However, less than a year after that admissions' interview, I was sitting in a meeting with him providing us with excuses and a sob story as to why he was on a probationary status. That was not all; a few months later, after the conclusion of the spring semester, he requested additional bonus assignments because he had not reached the threshold to leave probationary status. I read his additional essay and wondered if the principles we strive to instill will ever be absorbed. In the essay, he outlined strategies, which were impractical and unattainable. Included in those strategies was a plan for an accountability partner *outside the program*. An accountability partner is excellent, but one outside of our rigorous cohort is impractical. Another plan was to complete all assignments two weeks in advance. This is unfeasible due to the nature of our program with the massive quantities of group work and the need to balance group meetings with class and graduate assistantships.

This young man has tested my mettle as an instructor and as an individual, but he is a child of God and he is due the same respect that all the students should receive. I admit that my patience has reached new heights in working with him and it has made me more effectual as an instructor. I know that not all my students will be stellar and that many will try me to a point that I will undoubtedly have to profess in a manner they can understand in order to reach them. I know that these practical experiences added to my proverbial toolkit will prepare me for the challenges ahead when they arise.

Confessions of A High School Marketing Teacher: Teaching Is …

By Stefanie Samuel

PAIN … When a student says I'm late because my mom and dad were in a fight and I spent all night in the hospital nursing my mom's wounds.

HUMOR … When you see engaged students playing a game and learning, reasoning, joking, and laughing in harmony despite their internal or external differences and conflicts.

JOY …When you see the success of lessons taught and hear those beautiful rewarding words "class done already? That was fast" and eagerness to finish projects to see confidence light up the room.

ANGER …When you try to help a student who makes bad decisions, motivate him to value education, to hear he dropped out without a care for his future because too many give up on him.

DREARINESS … When administration provides no support, resources, materials, or natural affection for teachers or students and fills hallways and classrooms with empty promises.

EPIPHANY …When you disregard dreariness and see the success and rewards of the students and make roses out of concrete soil.

WORLD BUILDING … Where pieces of you (graduated students) are succeeding in the US, Caribbean, Asia, Europe.

DESIGN … When we produce lifelong lessons for engaged learning and life application. We tear down boundaries that mask as obstacles and setbacks.

Yes, this traditional profession is undervalued, overworked, beyond draining, but is an overwhelmingly rewarding job that redefines all life and teaching itself.

My Wondering

By Jesus Espinosa

What do I wonder about in respect to the students I teach?

In my class, I have students with several types of learning abilities. My concern is more with the ones who cannot read at their age level, yet their Individual Educational Plan doesn't explain it. To add more to this problem, the paraprofessional assigned to these students does not have a clue or knowledge about the subject matter, compounding the problem.

On a whole, I think that for those students time is quickly closing in on them, if it hasn't already. Today or tomorrow we will all be taking orders from a generation of people who went through the education process without being able to read, write, or spell properly. How are we to bridge the gap if we can't fix the problem of reaching out to those students who are less fortunate in the learning process? The question that comes to mind is: Can we redefine the real disadvantaged learner?

In recent years we have seen, heard or even read where people in high positions in society were perceived to have had learning disabilities. One good example was that of the former president, George W. Bush. If this was or is the case, then when will the leaders who continue to point fingers at teachers find a way to help facilitate an approach that everyone would accept?

One of the most damaging images is of professional athletes who may go through college without learning anything on their own except the sports they are good at playing. A good example of that was Dexter Manley, of the Washington Redskins Football team, who was offered a contract worth millions of dollars, more than he originally made, but didn't know what to sign because he could not read what was asked of him.

Again and again we, as educators, are confronted with the tasks of how to better teach or reach students with different learning abilities, and do this without the full support and guidance of those in charge who should know better. My Passion is to teach, not to be persuaded not to.

I Coming Over...

By Rhudel James

The first period class was almost over. There were just a few minutes left to remind the students about the deadline for the homework assignment. Although additional information was being given, many of them had already begun making preparations to leave for the second period class. As I walked around the room collecting calculators, I noticed one young man was excitedly reading the words written on a small piece of paper. It was no surprise that this student was unaware that his teacher was standing directly behind him, reading the very message that had his full attention. He was mesmerized!

This was not the first time that I had come across a "questionable" note passed among students. I confiscated the paper from that student and planned to confront him about its contents when the dismissal bell sounded. He was in truth, saved by the bell, at least for the moment.

The note read, "I cumin over 2 put the workin on u" and was from a sixteen year old male to a fourteen –year- old female. Now, I don't know if the intended receiver ever got to see this note, but I do know that the student I took it from wasn't the author of the message. In my estimation, "workin on u" was a sexual suggestion of what the boy wanted the girl to know and agree to. My concern was that because I knew both students very well, the possibility and probability of something sexual happening between them was almost 100%. Something might have already happened. I hoped not!

Do I speak with the author and conduct a morality check? Do I take a chill pill and accept the reality of "It is what it is"? Does it matter at all?

Maybe I was making too much of this little note. Was there anything really wrong with a suggestive note between classmates? Honestly speaking, hadn't we all as children done questionable things?

Educators, parents, family members, the community, business owners and legislators are all part of a child's village. We share the burden of raising our children to be respectful, productive and honest, law-abiding citizens. We all are on the front lines in the battle for the creativity, morals, souls, dollars and votes of this generation. The children themselves may not be aware of this, but we know this to be the truth.

Whether we agree or not, they mimic our behavior, follow our lead and become our mirror images. Through our daily interaction with this population, our positive and negative contributions in their lives significantly affect their mental, physical and spiritual growth. The quality of life experienced by these children is dependent upon how seriously we accept this tremendous responsibility. What we say and do affect their decision-making ability. Our input matters.

As an educator, I have personally chosen to respond directly to the "questionable" words, notes and behavior of my students about 75% of the time. To many of these students, I know that we are authority figures, confidants, role models, and sources of information. They look to us for appreciation, correction, direction, and inspiration. Some of them depend on us for consistent stability in their lives.

In our effort to meet their need, our own sense of morality comes into question; who are we to set high moral standards for these young, impressionable versions of ourselves? Aren't we all truly capable of sin? Do we not learn from our mistakes?

While it is debatable whether or not we all accept correction, do we all not profit from being directed in positive ways?

What parent or teacher, when correcting the behavior of children and students, hasn't heard the classic response, "You're making a big deal out of something you know you did as a child?" In other words, they label us as hypocrites doing one thing, but saying another. The statement is valid, but with a difference. We aren't children anymore.

What our charges don't know is that when we did our "wrong" as children we knew what we were doing wasn't right. It was wrong; we admitted it and accepted the responsibility and consequences for the behavior. At that age, we didn't appreciate being punished.

We know that they "get it" (our attempt to prevent them from making the same mistakes we did), but in their "foolishness," they try to get back at us, defending themselves with daggers of guilt-producing statements. Our "little children" find creative ways to "hurt" us emotionally. As children, we did some of the same things too.

Some parents actually fall for this ploy and end up over-compensating for what they perceive as their failure to show adequate love for their children. Other responses such as, "You don't love me!"; "I'm going to run away!" and "You'll miss me when I'm dead!" are also used and are just as effective. Much to our hurt, we get caught up in the moment and react to their accusations and threats with humor, "old folk sayings," reverse psychology, sarcasm, and threats of our own.

"You're going to kill yourself! There will be one mouth less for me to feed!" "You're going to run away! Come! Let me help you pack, just to make sure you have clean underwear!"

"I don't love you! Do you think I would put up with all this; cooking for and feeding you, buying and washing your clothes, doctoring you when you're sick, if I didn't care?" "Would I not discipline you when needed and check up on you in school? Did I not spend time with you and give you everything? Would I do all of this if I didn't love you!?"

These "words of wisdom" passed down from our parents to us, and from us to our youth, sometimes backfire and create an even bigger problem. If we hadn't been practicing what we preached, our current attempts to corral and control our wayward children could be filled with frustration.

Perhaps the most popular "defense" put forth by our creative geniuses has been "You don't understand me!"

Imagine that! Despite all that we do for our children, some claim that we are "too old" to understand them and what they go through as young people today. Most of them clearly do not appreciate our stories of struggle when we were their ages. How do we respond to their assertions? We tell them more stories.

When they complain about us invading their space and having no privacy, we tell them about how our parents reminded us of who paid the rent/mortgage and who really ran things. We remind them of whose food they are eating and who transports them everywhere.

If they give us the "rolling of the eyes," we remind them of who brought them into this world and who can take them out. If they display other body language indicating the "I don't care to hear what you're saying!" attitude, we convey memories of whippings earned and describe the instruments used to get the messages into our heads.

When they fuss about not having name brand clothing and shoes, we tell them about our having to go to school wearing "hand me downs." If they suggest that we just don't understand their music, we start singing "old school" hits and explain the meaningful lyrics.

When they claim that they are vegetarians, yet don't want to eat their vegetables or don't like what we cook, we tell stories of our having to share three chicken wings among nine children or going to bed without eating, night after night.

When they complain about not having an allowance, we enlighten them about our having to work like slaves, doing house chores and odd jobs, just to get enough change to buy candy. Some of us learned the importance of "earning our keep" early in our lives. If we did well in school, we were able to get a little more money and go to the movies with our friends. For those families not struggling financially, rewards given to their children still came with a price.

If they dare compare their living conditions to that of their friends, we express our disappointment in their ungratefulness, not appreciating all that they have and all that we do for them, and oftentimes label them as being disrespectful.

Are we ignoring their concerns, feelings and thoughts? Are we being unfair to their point of view? Are we the reason for the anger, callousness, discontentment, and irreverence often displayed by this generation of youth? How can we expect our children to "do the right thing" if we don't show them in word and deed what "the right thing" is? Can we change their minds and reverse the negativity exhibited by their understated rebellion? Do we want to? The more serious question is; What if we don't?

To adequately answer the questions of what are we to do about saving our children from the destructive lives they might be leading or heading to, we need to clarify a few things. First of all, not all of our children are rebellious, disrespectful, or ungrateful. Thank God!

Many are honoring their parents by being productive, working and/or pursuing education/training, positively contributing to society. They are doing their best to be the leaders that they are and fulfill their dreams. We need to applaud them more than we do. We have somewhat ignored these obedient sons and daughters because we have been forced to focus on those who routinely defy rules and challenge our authority. Even the "good" ones sometimes rebel a bit just to get our attention.

A popular biblical verse, Proverbs 22:6 reads, "Train up a child in the way he should go: and when he is old, he will not depart from it." In another scripture, Luke 15: 11-32, a story is told about a prodigal son.

These two references serve well to explain how children, despite being raised under the same roof, by the same authority figures, can grow up to be virtual polar opposites; for example, one can become a police officer while the other chooses to become a criminal. Every child is unique and deserves the freedom to interpret life's lessons as he/she sees it. Every decision made is an option chosen by that individual.

Training involves the long-term and cumulative results of daily teachings. A doctor is considered trained in medicine after years of being taught (internships) in various classrooms. A martial artist is considered trained in martial arts after accumulating different color belts (levels) up to the black belt. When a child is older, there is the implied understanding that maturity has occurred. The time lived between being a child and being old (fully matured) is one of many adventures, experiments, growth, regrets and reconciliations.

The story of the prodigal son is the ultimate story of riches to rags and back to riches again. The riches were about having family values. This story tells of a child growing up in a wealthy family, demanding his inheritance and stepping out on his own, wasting it in a partying lifestyle, bottoming out, recognizing the error of his ways, finally reuniting with his family and being restored to his place of prominence within the family.

It tells of the "good" brother who stayed with and worked in the family business; of his not understanding how his father could welcome back and honor the unruly son, while he had never received as much as a token for his faithfulness. He was, in fact, appreciated by his father but felt neglected and disrespected by the father's show of affection.

What this "good" son wasn't mature enough at that time to understand was the fact that reconciliation is a time of celebration because "That which was lost, was now found." The return of the prodigal son to the security of the home is every parent's dreams realized and prayers answered.

There is no guarantee that if we raise our children in church, learning and doing the good and right things, that they will remain in the "light" and not venture into the "darkness." After we have done our best to bring up our children in the "fear" of God, all we can do is continue to do what we know to do; be available to them, pray for them, and be the ultimate examples of God's children as we have striven to be.

It is our right, obligation, privilege, and responsibility to police our own children. Without a doubt, our children are worth saving. Mistakes we've made in parenting can be corrected and we can still learn new ways to reach our children, even when they become adults.

Everything begins and ends with honesty. We can be honest and admit that at some point in our lives we had strayed away from the truth of God. We can and should believe what He has said about His loving us. We can "go back home again." Like the prodigal son, all of us have strayed, but because of God's faithfulness and our need for redemption, returning home to a place of security, love and blessings is the first step.

Being personally responsible and holding ourselves accountable is the best way to lead by example. Our children have been watching and learning our ways from birth and without a doctorate can tell us who we are. They know enough of the ugly truths we have experienced, either by our admission or their observation. Some of our children are confident enough to tell us about ourselves, while others are content to remain silent witnesses. Developing an honest and respectful open line of communication with one another is the best way to know, be known and address future misunderstandings.

We need to applaud the efforts of our children refraining from spoiling them when they do well. Appreciating expected positive behavior is a good thing to do, but when they perform above what is required we ought to make a big deal about it; we should not only recognize them for negative behavior. Doing as they are supposed to on a daily basis should be as natural as eating; we eat to live and children thrive when they are paid attention, rewarded, and stroked.

Our youth require consistent attention, discipline, encouragement, maintenance, recognition and much prayer. We cannot give up on them because they disrespect the law, themselves and even us, their parents. We shouldn't assume that they all don't know right from wrong and do whatever they please without regard to negative consequences. We would do well to remember how God's mercy prevailed over our own lives as we did "our mess" when we had the opportunity as immature and selfish people.

There are prisons and hellish times awaiting those choosing to become law-breakers and abusers of God's children. We can and should remind our young people that they can return home, to an environment where love is not a derogatory four letter word. When all else fails and they find themselves in an embarrassing or depressing situation, (prison or other confinement, homeless, unemployed, dead-end job, bad marriage or relationship, etc.), they need to know that someone loves and cares for them.

So, how did I respond to the "workin" note? I chose to ignore it at first due to having other things to do. It came to my attention later in the day when the young man got into trouble for saying something very inappropriate to a female teacher. I had no choice but to confront him on both counts.

During my planning period I sought out the young man, found where he was and brought him to my classroom. I was very direct with him and explained my position. This was not our first one-on-one counseling session, so he was used to my method of taking on the role of the concerned teacher/parent/coach. He was also one of my basketball players and was aware of my stance on the issue of disrespect.

This time I tried a different approach. After letting him know why I wanted to talk to him, I placed my hand on his shoulder, bowed my head and silently, began to pray. We sat there, without talking to one another, for another few minutes. I wondered if my plan was working.

Finally, after what might have felt like hours to him, he made a profound observation. He said, "I know you expect more from me. I am a good person, a good student and still a work in progress. I am worthy of the time you spend with me. I apologize for my bad decision to disrespect the teacher." As cheesy as that sounded, those words reflected the many conversations we previously shared. He was, in fact, listening.

I asked specifically about the note. Without hesitation, he responded, "She never saw the note, but I need a little help with that. She had been saying things to me in front of her friends, challenging me, and I wanted her to know that I wasn't afraid of her mouth. I wasn't going to go anywhere, just wanted her to think that I was."

I asked, "What if she called your bluff?"

"I planned to leave her hanging, to show her I could play with her mind just as she was trying to do with mine," he replied. I advised him of being true to himself and not getting caught up with getting back at or even with those who chose to be antagonistic.

Coincidently, I was able to share the details of the note with the girl's parent in a parental conference held for other reasons. I did this because I wanted this parent to be aware of the attention her daughter was commanding. I wanted this young lady to know that not all invitations were complimentary.

"I comin' over to do homework with you" might have been a more acceptable lyric, although highly unlikely and unrealistic.

Why Are You Still Teaching?

By Elizabeth Beck

Why do you continue to teach your students in the classroom the way that you do? Do you enter your classroom and teach from the textbook, assign work that is boring and irrelevant? Have you become too complacent? What can you do to excite your students and encourage them to learn simultaneously reenergizing yourselves? When was the last time you left the four walls of your classroom to make the connection between theory and reality? Or looked at a lesson from the student's perspective? When was the last time students were excited about your class, about school, or about life? Do you really care about your students and their future? Is your reason for remaining in the teaching profession to collect a paycheck?

As students enter your classroom whether for the first time or the twentieth time, are they excited to be there? What have you prepared for them today to make them eager to learn? Are you teaching the same way today as you did five years ago, ten years ago, or fifteen years ago? When you prepared today's lesson, were you genuinely interested in the selected approach? What new ideas or perspectives have you researched to implement in the classroom to bring forth positive energy and passion back into your lessons? When was the last time you opened a book to learn about current issues and trends? What information can you share with your co-workers that could enhance their teaching? What changes can you make this school year to bring about a transformation in yourself, your students, and your schools? How can you create positive, learning environments for your students and yourselves? Do even enjoy teaching?

As you reflect on your years of teaching, ask yourselves these questions, and turn to your co-workers and ask them the same. If you are unable to respond positively to these questions, I ask you ... *Why are you still teaching?*

Why Teach?

By Anny Prescott

Teach: "To impart knowledge or skill," "to instruct in," "to cause to learn by example."

Teaching is something I do not only for the money; I teach because of my love for children. I get great joy seeing the smile on my children's faces when they excel in their work. I not only teach academics, but some etiquette, social skills, also some Bible for good measure.

I love to give my children a pep talk or two every morning, sometimes twice daily. My goal for my children is not only to leave the class with academic skills, but to have pride and faith in themselves. I want them to hold their heads high, believing they will come out on top. They know that I believe in them because we all need someone to believe in us. They know they are the best, and they should always do their best. They also know that they will achieve anything they put their minds to. How do they know that? you ask. Because I tell them that. Being a good teacher requires me to go beyond books and into my children's world; I have to understand where they are. Teaching by the book sometimes is far beyond their reach, so I need to reach them before I could teach them.

I could remember my first volunteer teaching job: it was to get (Sandra) to spell and write her name; it was a struggle. We reached our goal months later. By the time June rolled around she was able to spell and write her first and last names: she smiled "Miss Prescott, I can spell and write my name." I teach, help, advise children not to be in the spotlight, but there's a reward I feel inside when they accomplish their goals. Teaching is like being a good mother; I take pride and joy in running my home and the classroom.

English as a Second Language

By Dalton L. Carty, Jr

"Meh son, mean no punk!" screamed Jahni. "I doan need to be no white man fo people to ovastand me. Mean ga tak or ac like one."

Mr. Roberts was shocked. In thirty years of teaching, he had never encountered such impudence. He retorted, "I don't want to make you a white man, Mr. Bellows. However, I do want you to comprehend the rules of proper diction and prose. As your English teacher, it is my job. I only wanted you to correctly pronounce the words you were reading."

Mr. Roberts gazed at the fourteen-year-old 7th grader in hopes of quelling his anger. He didn't know what infuriated the usually compliant Jahni. He only asked him to properly pronounce words from the chapter the class was reading.

Yet, the tactic failed. The boy quipped, "All a yo com here an wan people to wak deh white man path. Buh it ain goan work wid me. I's a Thomian and I goan stay a Thomian. Mean care what yo or anybody say."

Rising from his desk and advancing towards the youngster, Mr. Roberts decided Jahni Bellows needed a conference with the principal. "You must see Mr. Regan," he said. "I will not tolerate your disrespect." Standing in front of Jahni, the tall, lean Tortolan grasped the juvenile's forearm and escorted him to the principal's office. Telling the class to silently read the remainder of chapter 20 as the door closed, teacher and pupil walked briskly to the heart of the facility where Mr. Regan sat quietly in his office. He listened to Roberts's account of what had transpired and then turned to Jahni. "What's the matter with you?" Mr. Regan inquired. "Why did you behave that way towards Mr. Roberts?"

The lanky teen paused a few minutes as his big brown eyes evaded Mr. Regan's hard glance. Jahni's dark, handsome face seemed cold and his manner defiant. Suddenly, as if a response had just emerged in his brain, Jahni hotly answered, "Look, all I know is dat dis man wan tell me dat I ga tak an ac like a white man in his class. Mean in dat."

Regan was stunned. He said, "First, this man has a name and you will use it. Second, Mr. Roberts teaches English and, if he says that you are to speak, write, or behave in a certain manner, you must comply."

"Mean in dat. I been speakin like dis since I wuh barn and mean goan change now. So, if you goan suspend me, do it and leh me go!" Jahni blurted. Mr. Regan agreed. He called Jahni's house and his Aunt Velma answered.

"Hello," she said. Regan proceeded to explain the situation to the woman. Velma wailed, "God give me strength! That boy will be the end of me." Although they could not decipher what she was saying, Mr. Roberts and Jahni heard Velma on the phone as her demeanor went from calm to erratic. The latter appeared indifferent as he stood like a solid coconut tree listening to his aunt's sobs.

She continued, "Mr. Regan, Jahni's mother recently passed away and since then the boy has been a constant headache. We have no family on St. Thomas. I am a single mother on welfare with my own four children. I have another sister, Tilda, in Colorado and we have discussed Jahni moving there to live with her. She's single and has no children. In fact, she called this morning to say he could go back with her next week after the funeral. She's arriving tomorrow. She wants Jahni to promise that he will behave and study hard. However, Jahni does not want to go and has refused to accept the inevitable."

The staunch stare on Mr. Reagan's face melted as he discerned the debacle of the boy and his family. He said, "My condolence on your sister's passing. I had no idea that that had happened."

Upon hearing of a death in his student's family, Mr. Roberts instantly spun and watched Jahni, who remained unshaken. Roberts deduced the event must have been the cause of his student's recent hostility. Yet, he didn't understand why. What did proper pronunciation have to do with Jahni's frustration? He figured Mr. Regan would furnish greater insight once the conversation with the young man's relative was over.

Regan persisted, "I know things are hard for you and Jahni. However, he was disrespectful to Mr. Roberts and I wondered if you have someone who could pick him up. I will suspend him for the remainder of the week and you both can try to work things out."

"All right, Mr. Regan.," Velma said. "I will ask my neighbor, Mrs. Quinn, to pick up Jahni. Yet, he may not return to school next week because he could be in Colorado."

Regan stated, "Fine. Please ask Mrs. Quinn to come immediately."

"OK. Thank you for all your help, Mr. Regan. Tell Mr. Roberts I apologize for Jahni's rudeness," she said.

"Very well. Again, condolence on your sister. If there is anything I could do to assist, please let me know. Goodbye."

Mr. Regan hung up the phone with a disgusted thump and a deep sigh. His hand held the receiver for several minutes before he lifted his great head and gazed at Jahni, who remained obstinate. Shaking his skull, Mr. Regan exclaimed, "Boy! Why are you misbehaving? Don't you realize that woman is doing all she can to help you grapple with your mother's death?"

Jahni only frowned and shifted to the side in an attempt to escape Regan's words. Mr. Roberts, wide-eyed, pivoted towards the long legged child. Then, Regan stood with his arms straight and fists taut on his ample cherry wood desk.

He asserted, "You should be helping her, not cursing your teachers. Can you imagine how difficult your mother's death is for her? She has four children to rear and now she has to deal with your selfish attitude!"

Mr. Roberts inserted, "Jahni, I'm sorry about your mother's passing. I know it must be inconceivable. However, why should it make you angry at proper pronunciation?"

Jahni merely rolled his eyes and sucked his teeth at these words of comfort from the man who caused his secret to be divulged.

"Mr. Roberts, don't stress. He will comprehend the need for an extensive vocabulary and decent diction when he moves to Colorado to live with his aunt. He'll see how challenging it is to make friends or get a job when no one understands what he says," Mr. Regan suggested as he retook his seat.

With an astonished look, Mr. Roberts replied, "Mr. Regan, that may be the root of the problem. He may be apprehensive about leaving home for an unfamiliar place where he won't fit in."

Roberts continued, "In Tortola, we have the same problem with foreigners like Hispanics who arrive and don't speak much English. They become angry and disgruntled due to their inability to speak proficient English. Some engage in crime because they feel they lack options for finding work or acquaintances.

Nodding in agreement, Mr. Regan added, "Correct. We've had that problem with many Hispanic and Haitian students. Yet, this boy was born and raised locally. He shouldn't have problems with English. It's the only language he knows."

Roberts countered, "That's only partially true, Mr. Regan. These youngsters learn Creole long before they grasp proper English. Caribbean dialects, with their broken semantics and discombobulated syntax, are established languages. They are spoken in our homes and the first sounds children hear. Thus, juveniles internalize such verbal cues prior to acclimatizing standard speech."

Regan agreed. He said, "Again, I concur. However, he's been in school for seven or eight years. If he can't distinguish between proper and improper grammar, it's not our fault. That is, his parents and previous teachers must share the blame. They needed to ensure he knew the difference. Students must recognize English, not dialect, is the official language of the territory. It is what we use to evaluate them and what colleges will use when they apply."

Roberts affirmed, "You have a point. Tortolan students speak very well and most don't have problems code switching. Yet, here in the USVI, changing between local dialect and standard English appears to be a profound issue. It's like English is a second language for natives."

Regan said, "Exactly! However, English as a second language or ESL is a course expressly designed for immigrants. If we require an ESL class for natives, the government should change the official language from English to territorial dialect. As a U.S. territory, I doubt that will happen. Moreover, dialect has significant deficiencies. It lacks organization, integration, standardization, and international acceptance. Lastly, St. Croix has a totally opposite dialect than St. Thomas. Hence, society can't agree on correct speech within the territory, let alone beyond it."

Roberts suggested, "That may be. Still, it's the territory and local educators who look idiotic when kids leave for some distant locale and can't speak, read, or write standard English. That fact is complicated because the V.I. is an American territory and English is the official language."

Regan uttered, "Well, that's a conundrum for government and society. Jahni said he always spoke in dialect and he didn't need to act like a white man to be understood. If society and government are concerned about how they are perceived by foreigners, they should augment their ideals. I am not saying to abolish dialect because that is one aspect that makes the Caribbean, including the American Virgin Islands, unique. Yet, the demand for improved English skills must be a priority if students are to be successful."

Roberts acknowledged, "The demand is exacerbated when students travel off-island for school. They must grasp basic English rules as to not make themselves or the territory appear inept."

During the intense exchange between administrator and subordinate, Jahni had taken a seat and was perplexed by the discourse. His expression softened as he listened to the men talk. He tried to follow Regan and Roberts, but was lost at the introduction of unfamiliar terms like code switching.

"What St. Thomian tak ga to do with English? Aint deh da same?" he finally questioned with a puzzled look.

Roberts answered, "That is the quandary. You children believe dialect is English and don't fathom the distinction between the two. You speak, write, and read dialect rather than English. What's more, you think it's appropriate because you know English is the language of the U.S.V.I. Thus, you use horrible grammar because you feel it's good English."

"Buh dat's how we tak. Eh can be wrong. We speek English an it's as good as any White man lingo," Jahni asserted.

Regan confessed, "That is how you comprehend the situation. But low English grades say otherwise. Locals want to preserve culture, but, in the process, they hinder acquisition of skills necessary for academic and professional achievement."

Jahni gasped, "Yo sayin, I really will ga trouble speakin and ovastandin dem white people in Colorado! Buh wha I suppose to do? I din know that we duh speek bad. I been speakin like dis since I wuh small. Wha I suppose to do."

Realizing the child's fear, Roberts said tenderly, "Jahni I know you are frightened. Perhaps that will aid you in perfecting your speech and grammar. You were always inclined to participate in class whenever I called on you, but now you must try to develop a keener cognition of English if you are to succeed on the mainland. What's more, you must relinquish the hostility from your mother's death. People are more disposed to help an obedient youngster than a disagreeable one. Do you understand?"

"Yeah," he said. "Buh dis been such a big shock to me. I mean fus my mothda die and leave me wid my aunt. Den, she tell me she caan afford to care fo me along wid she fo chilren. So, she say she goan call me Aunt Tilda, who mean see in years, to see if I co live wid she. I ga leave my home an friends to go to a place I neva been befo. I ga change deh way I tak so white people co ovastand and I doan stay alone fo deh rest of my life. Buh I already alone and the deh one person who love me ain coming back."

As Jahni said this, a few tears began to trickle down his face. He turned from Roberts and Regan. However, they saw the boy's anguish and felt for him. As they watched the adolescent, he began to sob profusely. To mask his pain, Jahni's long, veined hands met his slender, brown visage as cries emerged from his tortured soul. Asking repeatedly, "Why me?" he wept openly as though it was the first time he was grieving for his mother and himself.

Roberts kneeled by the juvenile and caressed the same forearm he used to lead him to the office when their confrontation commenced. In a low voice, he said, "Son, I know this must seem like the hardest time in your short life. But God doesn't give anyone more than he can bear. You can and will survive this ordeal. However, you must decide how to do that. You can comprehend the predicament and persevere, or allow it to ruin you and tarnish all your mother desired. Only you can make the choice. Finally, always remember there are people who love you like your aunts. Mr. Regan and I also care and will always be there if you need help. You only need to call. Don't perceive this as the end of your life, but the beginning of a totally new chapter you can script anyway you choose. Now stop crying and wipe your face. Mrs. Quinn should be waiting outside."

Roberts handed the boy a napkin which he used to clear his wet eyes. He helped him rise to his feet and gave him a small tag.

Roberts said, "This is my card. It has my home and cell numbers. If you don't come back to school next week and can't stop to say goodbye, call me anytime you need to talk even if just to say hi. If you don't reach me, leave a message. I promise I will return the call. Yet, don't leave angry. You're still young with the future ahead. Your mother wanted the best for you and I will try to help you achieve it. Although I am your English teacher, I could also be your friend. But you must attempt to help yourself. Don't disrespect teachers or cause trouble for relatives. Work hard and everything will be fine."

Jahni didn't know what to think. He appreciated what Roberts said, but he was still nervous. This was a big move. Nonetheless, he shook Roberts's and Regan's hands before he left. He thanked them and opened the door to meet a short, middle-aged woman seated in the office.

"Jahni," she said as she stood. "You should know better than to get into trouble with all that has occurred recently."

"I know, Mrs. Quinn. Leh go," he replied.

He never returned or called Mr. Roberts for advice. Weeks later, Roberts eventually investigated the boy's whereabouts with relatives, but decided not to contact him because he felt Jahni needed to accept himself and society before seeking assistance; to come to terms with his suffering and grief. He hoped that was the case for him in Colorado, but he never heard from the boy again.

Just Not Interested?

By Charlene Spencer

I stood at the classroom door as 21 ninth graders rushed noisily past. "Yeah, I'm out of jail!" one girl exclaimed, and went to join a friend leaning against a column in the bustling hallway. She smiled and chatted with the other girl, the pleats on her plaid skirt opening and closing like an accordion as she blithely shifted her weight in delightful freedom.

"I thought you were worried that you'd be late for your next class," I called out. "You will be if you don't hurry."

"But I don't have class," she sniggered. "I don't have a second period. I just wanted to get out of your class."

"So you came to class late; you refused to pay attention; you fretted that class was going overtime just so you could rush out to stand in the hallway! Why do you even come to school?" I asked, not really wanting to entertain her pitiable response.

A mere three months into my new profession, yet I had posited the question with a certain resignation, battle fatigue, and promptly shut the door. Her mother and sister had come just a few weeks ago to inquire of her progress. They were bemoaning late breaking news that the ninth grader had been gallivanting in the local shopping center during school hours.

"Girlie!*" they had pled with her there, just outside the door. But she said nothing and seemed at most bothered by the appeals, the coaxing, the fuss.

"So wha' if I failing nine grade. School boring!" she offered, finally.

Following formative evaluation exercises, I had been earlier persuaded by her apparent grasp of basic concepts. Despite her tardiness and general non-compliance, Girlie seemed to be performing adequately-- a thing at which I marvelled— that is, until the day I moved her to another seat because of her incessant chatter and discovered that, in her new location, she could not demonstrate the same level of competence.

Today, two hours past final exams, it is evident that neither my words of encouragement nor her family's, nor study sheets, nor makeup assignments opportunities, have had any measurable good effect.

I guess I'll have to try again next year.

*A pseudonym

Student Mediocrity

By Joan Paulus

As a classroom teacher of reading on the high school level, an area of great concern for me is the student mediocrity syndrome that persists on the part of many of the students. Let me try to clarify this terminology. Student mediocrity refers to the attitude embraced by students of performing sufficient tasks or assignments to just get by. This is particularly evident by their choosing to settle for C's when they have the capacity to produce "A" work. To put it more succinctly, students are not working to their fullest potential. I believe there are several factors which seem to contribute to this phenomenon, namely: peer pressure, the need for acceptance and belonging, low expectations, and an insufficiently cultivated ambiance for achieving.

Peer pressure is tough. Even in friendships I have witnessed academically inclined students succumb to peer pressure in defense of a "friend" who was ill prepared, disrespectful to the authority, or just did not complete an assigned task. The more academically inclined student became the one to attack authority rather than encourage and guide his classmate on the road to success. He fights rather than points the way and usually ends up giving in to negativity along with his peers. This is a recurrent scenario among our students whereby values seem askew.

Another side of peer pressure is that in which students collectively attempt to exert pressure to cause the one in authority to allow for laxity which they believe is to their advantage. This is evidenced by deliberately not being prepared and on time for tests, assignments, or even classes. Some resort to procrastination which becomes detrimental to their overall growth and productivity, especially when timeliness is a criterion for assessment. Mob psychology is applied in the hope that standards will be dropped to accommodate their developing skills and habits.

The need for acceptance and belonging is the second factor that is especially prevalent among new and incoming students to the public school system. Being in an unfamiliar environment brings its own set of challenges. I have seen new students attach themselves to others who were very much in need of guidance and did not serve as good role models. Sometimes a student can lose an entire year just trying to adjust to the curricular demands and expectations while trying to fill the need for a sense of acceptance and belonging.

The third level of student mediocrity is that of low expectations on the part of the student himself. A student with shattered dreams and hopes usually puts little effort into his assignments. Economic pressures on family life can, at times, render a student hopeless to the impending future. Negativity often pervades his thoughts: "Why dream? Why hope? My parents did not make it, so who is to say I will? I don't even have a bank account, so why think of further studies? Who will foot the bill?" A lack of sufficient economic resources can be a cause for stress and anxiety which is often played out in low self- esteem and expectations.

The fourth aspect is that of an insufficiently cultivated ambiance for achieving. Schools are making strides in this area, but more efforts are needed to counteract the plethora of negative values which students tend to embrace as being the acceptable modes of conduct. The prolific use of obscenities, disrespect for fellow students and authority figures, fighting, cursing are all behaviors that do not promote a healthy and safe atmosphere which is conducive to achieving.

Confronted with these observations, how can I inspire students in my classroom to work to their fullest potential? What strategies can be implemented to address this situation? With these questions in mind, I am curious to find out what research suggests.

Students Achieving Higher Academic Standards

By Victor Barnes

I can be passionate about almost anything; anything that I am involved in is something that I give as much as I have. My passion is spread over three areas of focus: my relationships, my work, and my hobbies. If there is anything that you would regard as important, it would most likely fall in one of the three categories.

I will not go into my passion about my family. I would love to go into my passion towards soccer, or perhaps about high fidelity home speaker systems. I chose, however, to speak about my work because I think it is of more relevance to the audience as well as to bring into focus an issue that, as passionate as it may be, it is also a source of concern for me.

My passion regarding my work is based on my belief that whatever I do, I must do not necessarily to perfection, but I must do it to the best of my ability. My passion is about driving my students towards realizing their highest academic achievement levels. My passion is about academic excellence.

A current and popular line of thought seems to say that high academic achievement is no longer a major measure of a student's preparedness for facing the challenges of tomorrow's world. I differ. I still think that a strong academic base is fundamental to any further development of the mind as well as for a clear thinking process. It is a strong academic base that will yield the complete, rational and competent person who is not solely a consumer in tomorrow's world, but that this person should strive to become one of the few who dictate the lifestyles of thousands or even millions of consumers. The two, a person's level of higher academic achievement, and his level of comparative lower consumerism, are related. To the extent that a human is solely a consumer, which I interpret as a form of commercial enslavement, will soon become a strong indicator of his/her lower level of independent thought.

I believe that the newly designed trend is to create a world where we are mostly educated to a functional level. I strongly believe that there is an underlying new movement in education that is designed to create consumers of the great mass of the population. There is this new focus to have us up to date on the latest technological advancements. I am sure that not many of our students ever stop to think of the years of design work and expertise that go into any of the technology product that they see as ordinary, common, and a must have. It does not take mathematical, analytical or any of the higher order academic skills to be fully conversant with today's latest technologies. In fact, you do not have to be beyond basic literacy to have these technologies serve your daily needs.

So how does my passion relate to all of this? I believe that in tomorrow's world, if we are not able to produce even the technology that we need then we are going to be enslaved at the hands of a few. These few, which could comprise a few nations, or a few organizations, could so empower themselves intellectually, that they may soon be able to exert their dominance in the world in much the same way as strong military powers will protect their own land and people today. One should also note, if there is any hint of truth in the shifting of intellectual prowess, that the few who will actually hold the keys to our future are actually the ones who are currently targeting for themselves the highest academic achievement possible. Their primary endeavor at this stage is not to equip themselves with the latest technological gadgetry; rather their focus is to be fully conversant with the technology, and to use it to plan a more long-term goal aimed towards their sustainable future.

Having stated my views on the shift in power, I will return to the student in the classroom. The classroom is the primary zone for any future social design. There are those who are advocating that all students have the ability to learn, and I say too that all students can learn. But I believe that the classroom must be used for discriminating between the slow learner, the ordinary learner and the gifted learner. The level of highest achievement for each is different and it should be the teacher's prerogative to push each student to his/her highest level of attainment. Hence I will put the argument that if 70% is the lowest pass, and there is a class containing all three categories of students, an exam for the group should be so structured that the gifted student must work hard for a deserved 100%. It is the responsibility of the slow learner to earn a hard-fought 70%. Essentially the grades must be used to discriminate between good, better, and the best with an allocation zone also for the nonperformers, if they exist. In so doing, our good best will know that they are not just ordinary and will start to appreciate that "to whom much is given much is expected."

I will try to explain again how my passion for high academic achievement relates to an ordinary life. Absolutely no decision in one's life should be left to that person's whims and fancies. All decisions must be controlled. Within that controlled environs, there must be space reserved for one's wishes and dreams; the world of fantasy acts as a reservoir for keeping thoughts alive. The academic training is useful in that it helps us to rationalize before we make conscious decisions. As a matter of arguing, one could say that we do not have to be schooled to make rational decisions. True, because even in an informal social setting, we must acknowledge that lessons are learned as we interact, and it is from the lesson that we project our conscious acts. School is only a medium for formally imparting some of the lessons that we need to make our lives and community a more enriched and accommodating environs. But the major advantage that the school offers over ordinary social interactions is that the school offers a designed plan of activities, and if this plan is carried out effectively, when applied properly it will act to protect the interest of the community. School is important because it helps us to make decisions for our personal social wellbeing as well as for the good of the community.

A rigorous training of the mind, both in school and otherwise, will bring our mind to act upon all conscious thoughts before they are manifested. Rigorous training results in an inquiring mind. What are some of the components that I look for in a well prepared/learned/ excellent student?

An excellent student is one who has mastered the contents of the relevant subject area. Mastery by itself indicates that the student would have dedicated the time needed to cover both width and depth of the subject area. Mastery involves a planned approach to attain a particular outcome. For mastery there has to be fine tuning loops along the pathway to the designed outcome. The more rigorous and demanding the subject area, then the more complex and interwoven will the pathway to mastery become. Along this pathway there is no room for frivolous affairs, and trivial pursuits leading back to the starting point. This points to a student who is not afraid of making mistakes. He learns from his mistakes and is not discouraged by them.

There may be no perfect decision in the human life. There can be poor decisions. If we can evaluate circumstances around us, we should end up with decisions that are better for us. High academic achievements do not, by themselves, make us arrive at better personal choices. What they do is that they inform the decision making processes and allow us to better understand the interaction of variables that will lead to our present situation. A properly trained mind will methodically seek to reverse a bad decision or will tend to halt a repeat of a previous bad decision.

There are many cases of casual observations that I may have used as support in favor of my passionate stance on maximum academic achievement for my students. And, although my own case would be a poor example to validate my passion and the reasons for it, I find that the greatest support for my inspirations towards my passion arises when I reflect on my own ancient educational process against the new thoughts and trends in today's educational process.

Drastic Measures

By Joan Paulus

With my entire teacher training on humanizing education, aesthetic education, Children Learn What They Live mantras, talking to students respectfully, I never imagined myself using obscenities in the classroom. What do you do with a rambunctious group of eighth graders whose speech is riddled with obscenities and take pleasure in seeing you cringe every time you hear one? Speaking gently to them did not stop the behavior. As a matter of fact, the undesired language increased.

As their remedial reading teacher, I hurriedly administered a reading test the following day only to discover that all eighteen students were at or above grade level. So what were they doing in my class? Upon consulting with the school principals, I was advised that these students were quite capable academically, but were repeaters. "They have had all the other teachers. We just need you to work with them the best way you can for the class period that they are assigned to you."

But how do I get them to listen, obey, and change their use of profanities? Prior to that school year, my teaching experience was on the elementary level, where I had taught all grade levels except kindergarten and sixth. This was my first junior high experience, and also my first with students who absolutely refused to comply with classroom rules and expectations.

I sought counsel from a neighboring teacher and former classmate who had been teaching at the school for a few years. Her advice to me was, "Sometimes you have to forget what you were taught was the best way to deal with a problem and just do the opposite. Sometimes you cannot be too nice."

The following day I greeted the students at the door and allowed the four that never used foul language to enter the room while the others were asked to wait outside. I greeted them, explained what my plans were, apologized for my would-be behavior, and stressed the need for a change of behavior on the part of their classmates. I then allowed those outside to enter and with the passage of each one, I directed the same foul language I heard them using in my class and on campus. For the first time there was complete silence. Mouths were hung open in disbelief. They probably thought I was crazy.

I let some time pass and then I asked, "How did I sound?" There was no response. I repeated the question two more times, but still no one answered. I then called on two individual students by name and repeated the question. Both responses were, "You did not sound good? Ms. Paulus." "Why did I not sound good," I prodded. "Because you used obscenities," was the class response. "Can you now imagine what it sounds like to me when you walk in my class using profanities?"

On a few occasions afterwards, a profanity or two did slip out, but they were followed by immediate apologies to the teacher and the students. I started to enjoy this class largely because we were learning to listen and learn from each other. Based on their concerns, I created a curriculum and we were able to address the fear of being promoted to a higher grade in a larger school with its many challenges. They were all promoted to the ninth grade that year. These students really made me love the teaching profession. I will never forget them. They are adults now with children and grandchildren of their own, and I am tickled when they greet me with a hug or a kiss and introduce me to their offspring or friend as their "favorite teacher."

Whipped

By Mary Jo Wilder

The stalking begins in Michigan. I get a text at my son's graduation under the wooden Superior Dome.

"Ms. Wilder I need a letter of recommendation." And as the kids say, I wonder, "Who dis be?" There is no name.

A student? I can't believe it. Grades are in. Class is over. However, when I go to respond, my antiquated droid drops the message. Swoosh, gone! Good thing. My baby, all grown up, is marching across the stage. The next day, I get another voicemail from the student, I hear Keyana's name, but the message is garbled, and my phone doesn't record her number. There are several more voicemails, on and off, throughout my trip, but she doesn't leave a contact number, so I can't call her back. She probably thinks I can't text either because I didn't respond the first time around. How bizarre this time is, the cell world, even with its imperfections, geographically linking, just about as far north as one can get in the states. She has no idea she is calling snow in the woods from sun and sand land.

I know people wonder why I'd give my students my cell number. Well in a moment of weakness, the latest round of incidents on island, I gave it out for emergencies because the office phone doesn't always work, and I just want to know if someone gets hurt. I don't like surprises, and I don't want to get mad at someone that has been absent yet again if it was because they buried a family member. I can get cranky if pushed too hard with "stupidness."

And this time, I got cranky with the stalking student, and no amount of walking and swimming brought relief this morning, so here I sit in the 200 year old something Moravian Church room for the A.A. noon meeting. While I wait for the facilitator to start, I remember it was the Moravians that came so long ago to teach the local people to read. Today, they house a program I have been checking into over the last ten years for moral support, working with at risk kids. My job titles and schools have changed, but the issues have not. Today I'm trying everything to lighten the load. I am not disappointed. The group, mostly able bodied men, have come from their jobs. They are clean, articulate, and funny, a nice change from the Friday night street people. Someone serves me coffee.

We read about the Tenth Step. How did they know? "Righteous anger, emotional hangovers, dry benders, criticism . . ." are to be avoided. I write in my little book, "Check yourself!" They move around the table, and I hear so many good things, my dis-ease is beginning to dissolve. We are human. We screw up. My turn comes, and everyone looks at me. As I've never come to this meeting before, I decide to share something.

I begin, "I needed this, I look around the table, I teach at the university, and I went off on a student. She wanted too much. I think I need to make amends."

I don't tell them about re-entry from up north, the missed flights, missed loved ones, missed preps, and start of summer session. I do share that a student came to my office after the umpteenth call wanting a letter for a Plaza Educational Scholarship, and I lost it.

However, I spare them the details. Yesterday, Keyana showed up at my office door. I was prepping, and multitasking, so I motioned her in and asked her what she needed. She explained the letter. Sorting through a new stack of papers, I asked her what she got as a grade in my class last semester; I forget everything once the grades are in.

"I got a D Ms. Wilder."

"What?" I respond incredulously. I think to myself; you got a D, and you want something from me?

I stop what I'm doing. I look for her file folder from last semester. I remember now the frustrating dropped calls I got up north. (Not her fault but frustrating just the same.) I read her grade summary sheet. O yes, she plagiarized a paper from the internet! She didn't finish the month long class research project. She didn't cite her sources. What? I'm furious! She intruded on my personal time with my son, and now she has taken me from prepping for my new class scheduled to begin in an hour to ask for a letter that was due yesterday. Really? When does it end? When is enough enough?

I am now boiling and spewing seven years of too many island favors; cleaning and painting classrooms, buying supplies, lost reimbursements, late contracts, no contract…. "Keyana, why should I recommend you?"

"I want to continue my education. I need the money for tuition."

I find two redeeming qualities. She has passed her writing labs. Good, many do not. She participated in our poetry festival and won an award. Ok.

"I am still angry. You missed a week. You didn't check in. You didn't finish up the class . . ." The young West Indian woman stands stoically erect and listens quietly. I end my tirade matching the beat of Robert Hayden's poem, "The Whipping":

The old woman across the way is whipping the boy again and shouting to the neighborhood her goodness and his wrongs.

… and spent, finally spent, I reluctantly agree to write the letter.

However, as soon as she leaves, I am aware I crossed a professional line, and the next day I get stuck in a poor me funk spiraling … which is why I'm where I need to be at the AA meeting with the guys on the 10th Step.

An hour later, I leave the church, lighter. I have heard all of the right things. My thoughts have shifted. I will make amends.

I go off to work.

I call her, "Keyana, I owe you an apology; I'm sorry I lost my temper with you yesterday."

"It's OK Ms. Wilder. I've written you a letter."

Sure enough as I open my door to the office, there is a big envelope on the floor. I pick it up and read….

I may not have accumulated grades to make me an A or B student but my time in your class will never be forgotten. When you asked me 'Why should I write this letter of recommendation for you Keyana?' I had no answer at the time, but I can now tell you that you were one of the few instructors who actually believed in me. You taught me things I now plan to apply.

I think, "O Lord," just like the local women I hear who say it so often. I repeat it again, aloud this time, in their cadence, "O Lord, give me the strength!"

A Soccer Story

By Cherrelle Herbert

"Hey Mel, have u seen the new kid?"

"No, Sarah. Why?"

"Melonie, that boy is cuuuuttttteeee!"

I laughed at Sarah's enthusiasm. That was typical Sarah. We were best friends and between the two of us, she was definitely the drama queen. In all honesty Sarah may just have been the most dramatic girl in our whole seventh grade class.

"Right Sarah. Every other boy is drop dead gorgeous to you. That's why your mom's convinced that the best thing to do with you is keep your boy crazy self grounded."

Sarah laughed, "That's not why I'm always grounded. I'm a free-spirit. She doesn't appreciate that."

I laughed.

The bell rang, I sat down, and as if on cue, Tyson Aron Rawlins entered the classroom.

I leaned over to Sarah and whispered. "He iiisssss good looking."

She leaned over to respond, "TOLD YOU!"

That was it. Love at first sight! I was head over heels for Tyson Rawlins.

A little later that day we were in health class and our teacher, Ms. Madison was trying to emphasize the importance of remaining fit.

"Another way to exercise is to participate in sports," she lectured. "Discuss with a partner ways in which you will remain active this school year."

Sarah slid her desk over to mine, "So what will it be?" She asked me. "Softball or volleyball?"

"Neither!" I responded. "I'm not athletic and I don't like sports."

"Oh come on," she pleaded. "Live a little."

"Nope. I'm good," I reiterated.

"All right class" said Ms. Madison. "Now I'm going to distribute sign up lists for some of the sports we have here on campus. If you commit to at least one sport you will only have to write one of the two final papers."

"Ugh!" I groaned. "That's totally unfair!" But I went over to the lists to determine which of the sports would be the lesser of the many evils.

In front of me stood Tyson. He was signing up for soccer.

"Hmmm…" I thought. "Soccer. Well at least if I'm going to be forced to warm the benches I might as well enjoy some eye candy." I quickly signed up for soccer and sat back down.

"So which one volleyball or softball?" Sarah asked anxiously.

"Neither," I said trying to stifle a smile.

"What? I don't get it. Didn't you just sign up for a sport?" She asked.

"Yes." I responded.

"Ok, so what did you sign up for?" She asked.

"Soccer!" I said.

"Soccer?" She repeted. "Sweety, there are NO girls on the soccer team. It's a co-ed team. You're just going to sit on the sidelines and rot."

"I know!" I said gladly. "And I'll get to admire Ty while I'm relaxing on the bench too."

Sarah laughed. "You are such a looser," she said. "Knowing you, you'll probably never talk to him anyways."

The bell rang and class was dismissed.

It was the first day of practice and I was miffed. Jogging, sprinting, sit-ups, push-ups, jumping jacks, stretches, who KNEW being a bench warmer would be so grueling.

"Ugh, " I moaned to myself. "This is def not what I had in mind."

I should have listened to my friend. I was the only girl on the team and the only one who wasn't enthusiastic about sports. By the time I got home, every muscle in my body hurt! I wanted to quit, but at the same time I didn't want to be a quitter. So I stuck it out.

Game day soon came and as expected, I warmed the bench. Tyson, however, was the star of the show, stealing the ball and scoring goals. I truly enjoyed my sideline seat on the bench.

The season progressed and I stuck with it, attending practice and warming the bench.

On the last game before the finals, I was happily sitting on the bench when my coach said: "Ok, Mel. Start warming up."

Oh great! I thought. The last thing I wanted was to get on the field, but a player was down and I guess I was the team's last resort so when the whistle blew I ran into position.

Luckily for me the game was over a minute later and I didn't have to do anything.

Before I knew it, the season was over and our team had won the championship!

I really never interacted with Ty, but at least I avoided a paper.

The next year we were asked to do the same thing. Sign up for a sport to avoid writing a paper. Tyson had moved away (his family was military I believe) and I had no motivation to go through that pain again.

Sarah came up to me. "Hey Mel. I was thinking of joining soccer. Will you be playing again this year?"

"Why would you want to play soccer?" I asked her.

"I think I'm in love with Clifford," she responded. "The Goalie."

I laughed. "LOOSER!" I said.

She laughed. "Come on Mel. If you join at least we won't be bored on the bench."

"Fine," I said. I signed up with my friend for another year of torture.

To my surprise, as the season progressed, I was becoming a fairly good soccer player; at least compared to Sarah anyway.

By the third game, my coach called me in to play and by the final games I was starting. I was enjoying the sport.

My ninth grade year I signed up for the team without being bribed or begged. That year I started every game and even decided to join a soccer club outside of school. That summer a recruiter asked me to play for a junior girl's VI national team. Excited by the prospect of traveling, I happily agreed to participate. The team took me to Haiti, Puerto Rico, the Cayman Islands, Trinidad, and the Dominican Republic. I was exposed to different people with different cultures all because I played soccer. I continued to play both at school and outside of school throughout my high school years.

Eventually I became a senior and began applying to colleges and universities.

That October, my father and I traveled around the US touring a variety of campuses and attending seminars. We got to DC and I decided to set up an interview at Georgetown.

"Melonie, I see here that you play soccer is that right?" asked the interviewer.

"Yes," I responded.

"What sparked your interest in soccer?" she asked.

"Weeeeellllll"

I began to tell her my story, why I joined the soccer team and what it led to. Throughout the story she smiled and even laughed.

At the end of the story she smiled and said, "Well, Melonie, that's quite the story."

Three weeks later I received the Early Action CONGRATULATIONS letter from Georgetown. Obviously the decision could not have been based solely on my Tyson/Soccer story; however, who knows if it helped?

"Well," Sarah said after I had told her the story and she congratulated me with a hug. "You didn't get Tyson, but you got Georgetown."

I laughed and responded: "I'd take Georgetown over Tyson any day. "

The ABCs of a Good Teacher

By Sharon Charles

A - Ask pertinent questions.
B - Believe that every child has the potential to learn.
C - Commit yourself to your tasks. Create a classroom atmosphere that is conducive to learning.
D - Diagnose students' strengths and weaknesses. Develop a good rapport with your students.
E - Engage students in meaningful and enjoyable learning activities. Encourage collaboration.
F - Formulate clear goals and objectives.
G - Guide students in making good decisions. Give thoughtful suggestions and clear directions.
H - Help students when they encounter difficulties.
I - Individualize instruction when necessary. Involve your students in critical thinking activities.
J - Join a professional organization.
K - Keep good records.
L - Listen carefully when students share their thoughts, opinions and ideas.
M - Model the type of behavior you expect of your students. Maintain a good relationship with students, staff and parents.
N - Note details.
O - Observe students' progress.
P - Praise students' efforts.
Q - Question inappropriate behavior.
R - Respect your students. Recognize special talents and gifts.
S - Seek opportunities for professional development. Set high expectations for your students.
T - Take time to know your students.
U - Understand individual differences in students.
V - Verify information before drawing conclusions.
W - Work diligently to accomplish your tasks.
X - Exercise control of your emotions. Experience the joy of teaching.
Y - Yearn for success. You can make a significant difference in the life of others.
Z - Zoom to do an outstanding job.

Dear Mr. and Mrs. Taylor

By Catherine J. John

Dear Mr. and Mrs. Taylor:

I would like to thank you for standing with me throughout the past months. I know that your wishes for Chloe were for her to go to med school and eventually return home to establish her private practice. As such, I experienced severe remorse when Chloe told me about the diagnosis. I was tremendously sorry that she had to withdraw from med school in order to be better positioned to deal with it, and I felt immense shame when I thought that I was the main reason that Chloe was faced with such a major decision. She expressed much regret when she spoke of the disappointment you would experience when she tells you of the situation. Chloe was also extremely concerned about the financial and medical insurance context within which the diagnosis was made.

Consequently, I have withdrawn from law school and have accepted a teaching position at a nearby high school. This provides a steady income. Additionally, when school closes for the summer, I will have several weeks to be with Chloe during the time she will require the most support. That time is quickly approaching, and we are both experiencing what I think is a moderate level of anxiety. Chloe's doctors have assured us that all look well and that we have no reason to be concerned.

I have enclosed copies of the most recent pictures. You can clearly see that you will be the grandparents of a beautiful little girl. We have named her Katherine Elizabeth. Chloe thinks naming our daughter after both of her grandmothers is a notable way of honoring our mothers and thanking them for standing with us in our choice. Enjoy the pictures. Sonogram technology has absolutely come a long way!

Sincerely,
Joshua

P.S. Chloe thinks the best wedding date is Christmas Day – six months after Katherine Elizabeth is born.

The Homework Dilemma: Writings from a Frustrated Teacher

By Lisa Beck

Dear Fairy Godteacher:

Today was not a good day. Most of the students in my class didn't do last night's math, English and science homework. I punished them by cancelling their recess time. They love that time to play and it hurts me to take away the one thing they love to do so much. If I don't punish them, they will not learn that when I assign homework, it is to be completed and turned in on time. ☹

I wonder why they didn't do their homework? It wasn't a lot. They just chose not to do it! Don't they realize that it is for their own good?!!! Homework has been assigned for years and it has helped many students; only good things come from doing homework. I don't know!!!! How can I get students to do their homework?

Signed,
Frustrated Teacher

Dear Frustrated Teacher:

The solution is not to punish the students for not doing their work, but to find out the challenges they face in doing the work. Look at what you are assigning for homework. Is it relevant to what they are learning, or is it busy work? Are you giving them enough time to complete the assignments or is it too much for the time allotted?

Signed,
Fairy Godteacher

Dear Fairy Godteacher:

It happened again!!!! No recess today! And, no, I didn't take your advice. These children must like missing recess. They didn't do their history or spelling homework last night. I guess that taking away recess is not the solution. I am getting very frustrated with these students! Why don't they do what they are told to do? The assignments are not a lot of work ... smh (shaking my head)! I need to find a way to encourage students to do their homework.

Signed,
Frustrated Teacher

Dear Frustrated Teacher:

Talk to other teachers who are having success with homework. Do research about homework assigning strategies and see what will work for your students. Do a self-check assessment to determine if what you are assigning is meaningful and relevant to the subject.

Signed,
Fairy Godteacher

Dear Fairy Godteacher:

Most of the students completed the homework, but it was only because they missed recess for a couple of days. The homework wasn't completed correctly and they complained the whole time we discussed the work. What is the secret to having students complete their homework and to do it well? Is this a problem all teachers face? What can I do to make some changes so that students want to do their homework, do it well, and turn it in on time? Even if they turn it in, are they learning or copying from each other? Is it worth it to assign homework or should I only assign in-class work and forget about homework? There has to be another way....

Signed,
Frustrated Teacher

Dear Frustrated Teacher:

There is no easy solution or quick fix. As I told you before, do the research; talk to colleagues, and do a self assessment on your homework assignment techniques. One strategy may work with one class and not another. Good luck and let me know how everything works out.

Signed,
Fairy Godteacher

Acknowledgments

Thanks to the members of the Editorial Committee:

Abigail Martyr and

Mary Jo Wilder.

Thanks to all those who suggested titles for the book, and those who voted in the selection of the title.

Thanks to all who submitted poetry and prose for the book.

Thanks to teachers everywhere!

About the Authors

- Victor Barnes teaches mathematics at the St. Croix Central High School. He is a Teacher Consultant of the Virgin Islands Writing Project.
- Elizabeth Beck is a teacher at the CTEC (Vocational School) at the St. Croix Educational Complex. She is a Teacher Consultant of the Virgin Islands Writing Project.
- Esther Burroughs teaches at the Juanita Gardine Elementary School. She is a Teacher Consultant of the Virgin Islands Writing Project.
- Lorraine Cadet teaches at the Juanita Gardine Elementary School. She is a Teacher Consultant of the Virgin Islands Writing Project.
- Dalton Carty, Jr. is a teacher at the Bertha C. Boschulte Middle School on St. Thomas. He is a Teacher Consultant of the Virgin Islands Writing Project.
- Sharon Charles, a teacher at the Lew Muckle Elementary School in St. Croix, has been an educator for more than 35 years. She is a co-director of the Virgin Islands Writing Project.
- Christopher Combie is a doctoral fellow at the University of South Florida in Tampa.
- Valerie Knowles Combie is an associate professor in the College of Liberal Arts and Social Sciences at the University of the Virgin Islands. She is the director of the Virgin Islands Writing Project.
- Mary Edwards is a recently retired English teacher on St. Thomas. She is a Teacher Consultant of the Virgin Islands Writing Project.
- Kimarie Engerman is a native of St. Croix, Virgin Islands. Currently, she is an Assistant Professor of Psychology at the University of the Virgin Islands.
- Jesus Espinosa teaches at the St. Croix Central High School. He is a Teacher Consultant of the Virgin Islands Writing Project.
- Denis Griffith is a Professor in the School of Education at the University of the Virgin Islands.
- Avril Hart is a recently retired teacher. She is a Teacher Consultant of the Virgin Islands Writing Project.
- Cherrelle Herbert was a Spanish teacher at the St. Croix Central High School when she wrote this story. She is a Teacher Consultant of the Virgin Islands Writing Project.
- Rhudel James is a special education teacher at the Youth Rehabilitation Center on St. Croix. He is a Teacher Consultant of the Virgin Islands Writing Project.
- Catherine John is a Teacher Consultant of the Virgin Islands Writing Project.

- Abigail Martyr teaches mathematics at the St. Croix Central High School. She is a Teacher Consultant of the Virgin Islands Writing Project.
- Nancy Morgan is an Associate Professor in the School of Education at the University of the Virgin Islands.
- Joan Paulus is a recently retired educator. She is a Teacher Consultant of the Virgin Islands Writing Project.
- Anny Prescott is a Teacher Consultant of the Virgin Islands Writing Project.
- Veronica V. Prescott is a Teacher Consultant with the Virgin Islands Writing Project, and is presently serving as the Tech Liaison. She is the Technology Integration Teacher at Juanita Gardine Elementary School.
- Rosalyn Rossignol is an Assistant Professor in the College of Liberal Arts and Social Sciences at the University of the Virgin Islands.
- Stefanie Samuel teaches at CTEC at the St. Croix Educational Complex. She is a Teacher Consultant of the Virgin Islands Writing Project.
- Camille Santiago is a high school teacher on St. Thomas. She is a Teacher Consultant of the Virgin Islands Writing Project.
- Charlene Spencer teaches English at the St. Croix Educational Complex. She is a Teacher Consultant of the Virgin Islands Writing Project.
- Mary Jo Wilder is an Assistant Professor in the College of Liberal Arts and Social Sciences at the University of the Virgin Islands.

We invite you to view the complete
selection of titles we publish at:

www.AspectBooks.com

Scan with your mobile
device to go directly
to our website.

Please write or email us your praises, reactions, or
thoughts about this or any other book we publish at:

P.O. Box 954
Ringgold, GA 30736

info@AspectBooks.com

Aspect Books titles may be purchased in bulk for
educational, business, fund-raising, or sales promotional use.
For information, please e-mail:

BulkSales@AspectBooks.com

Finally, if you are interested in seeing
your own book in print, please contact us at:

publishing@AspectBooks.com

We would be happy to review your manuscript for free.